BREATH OF LIFE
OR
KISS OF DEATH?

BREATH OF LIFE
OR
KISS OF DEATH?

YOUR VOICE AND YOUR PRESENTATION

JANET HOWD

Capriccio Press, London, 2002

BREATH OF LIFE OR KISS OF DEATH?
YOUR VOICE AND YOUR PRESENTATION

First published in Great Britain in 2002
by **Capriccio Press**

ISBN 0-9514835-2-8

Cover design by Kenneth Bentley
Book layout by randhdesign
Indexing by Angela Cottingham
Printed by South Ribble Printing Limited, Preston, England

Capriccio Press
10 St James Court
1 Marlborough Crescent
London W4 1HE

For China

ACKNOWLEDGEMENTS

Virginia and David Richards, Victoria Turner and Paul Terry read the manuscript
during its most shaky beginnings and made thoughtful and encouraging comments.
Gill Adams, Louise Turner and John Wakeford, and Robert Grafton Small
commented at later stages. Their insights added coherence to my method, rigour
to my wayward structure, and sensitively reined in my idiosyncratic style. Traces
of that remain, of course, because this little book, written to compliment the voice
and presentation skills workshops in which I deal so much with other people's right
to personal expression, is the expression of my authorship; so, all foibles are
definitely mine.

PREFACE

This slim volume is designed to encapsulate points and address problems which have come up time and time again during my voice and presentation skills workshops. The ideas you will find here have been tried and tested by people from all walks of life who had the courage to show and tell their concerns in front of others during those workshops and who, by doing so, enhanced the learning process both for each other and for me. I am grateful for that and hope that setting down many of the solutions we came up with will add to your skills and help you to give successful and enjoyable presentations.

If you wish to work in detail on matters of delivery and style you will find exercises to assist you and to trigger ideas which you can then expand for yourself. There are headings throughout the text which indicate the topics covered in the paragraphs beneath them – so you can skip bits you already know.

It would be ideal if you were able to video yourself from head to toe whenever you practise. If that is not possible, observe yourself in a mirror as you work – even watching your reflection in a window or a glass door is better than nothing.

Record your voice work. The voice you will hear on playback is likely to embarrass you. Nevertheless, do play it back, and do pay attention to it; even when the recording machine is of indifferent quality your recorded voice will be much more like the one which other people listen to everyday than is the one you *assume* they listen to everyday. Work to alter the voice that others hear rather than the one you hear in your head.

Aim to get over the discomfort of seeing and hearing yourself as quickly as you can. The longer such concerns remain uppermost in your mind, the longer it will take you to achieve the desired effects. Do not be surprised to discover that you feel extremely vulnerable as you undergo change.

The imaginative processes needed to learn new techniques can too easily be stultified by being set down on a page, so books are not ideal if they are to be the sole source of learning about practical matters. They can, however, point aspiring practitioners in the right direction. It is to this end – and because managers, sports coaches, professors, tour guides, barristers, teachers, doctors, and actors suggested that it would be helpful to refer to the methods we had discovered for breathing life into their presentations – that this book has been written.

CONTENTS

PART 1

YOU AND YOUR VOICE

You have your material prepared. You have done your homework and practised well. You are about to begin a presentation. Instead of feeling confident, you quiver inside. Fear grips your limbs and throat and threatens to sabotage all your careful planning. What's to be done?

You need an instant fix.

Breathe Out!

Squeeze as much breath out of your body as you possibly can.

Allow new, fresh air to travel deep down into your chest.

Breathe that air out, and as you do so, begin your presentation.

You have just got rid of stale air and replaced it with air full of oxygen. Fresh air is essential for a clear head, a steady nerve and a firm voice. In future, if you start to feel confused or out of control of your message or tired, or anxious, take a moment to squeeze out the stale stuff and make room for vital, energising, fresh air.

The adrenalin rush which we all sense when we are about to give a presentation signals to the body that there is an unusual job to be done. It heightens our awareness. But, sometimes the rush of adrenalin keys-up our systems too tightly and tunes up our voices to a point of strangulation. At such times the smooth-as-clockwork presentation we had prepared uncoils in a mass of quivering springs and the message which was supposed to hit its target like an arrow from a well strung bow turns to gobbledegook.

To avoid that happening, breathe out fully before you speak; consciously allow breath out from time to time during your presentation and deliberately breathe out before you deal with questions. You will then discover that you feel invigorated when the session is over no matter how complex its delivery turned out to be.

Then, when you are driving home or at home, when you are out partying or at work, when you are in front of your computer or watching TV, cooking a meal or washing up – even when you are in bed – consciously breathe out from time to time so that the breath which will automatically refill your vacated lungs can be a source of vitality to you for the rest of your life.

CONTROL YOUR BREATH

You may have found that squeezing out breath during that exercise also squeezed out phlegm and made you cough. In future you will find that the more often you 'flush' your wind-pipe with warm, outgoing breath, the less often you will experience a catch in the throat. You may also have found that taking in so deep a breath made you feel dizzy. To avoid that happening in future, we need to find out what taking in a deep breath really means.

Breathe evenly as you follow the steps outlined below.

Sit in an upright position and put the fingertips of both hands at the bottom of your breast bone. Notice where your breast bone ends and your fleshy stomach area begins.

Feel around the bottom of your ribs – each hand moving in opposite directions – all the way to the middle of your back until the fingertips of your right hand meet up with the fingertips of your left hand at your spine.

Take your hands away.

Open the palms of your hands and place them lightly, one on either side, and at the sides of your ribs.

Your thumbs should be facing forward and be in contact with your squashy waist, the rest of your fingers should be reaching round your bony rib cage towards the middle of your back.

Cup the lower part of your ribs on your right-hand side, in the palm of your right hand. Cup the lower part of your ribs on your left-hand side, in the palm of your left hand.

Squeeze breath out, and then breathe in.

Draw that new breath down so deeply into yourself, that you can feel it pushing your hands away from each other. (You don't need a lot of breath: just enough to feel that you can hold it, for a split second, between the palms of your two hands.)

Breathe out and allow your breath to flow as normal.

Drop your hands onto your lap, and whilst your body can still recall the feeling of where your hands had been, aim to draw breath down into that same space.

You should get a sense that the breath you take is travelling right down to your navel.

The instruction – "Take a deep breath" – means exactly what it says. It is not how much breath you take in but how deep down any amount of breath can sink inside you which will fuel good speech.

When you think you've got the hang of breathing so deeply, stand up as if you were about to give a presentation, and repeat all the exercises outlined above.

Most of us discover that breathing so deeply is an unusual thing to do. Most of us allow breath to travel only half way down inside our chests. Large amounts of air trapped in so shallow a space cause us to feel clogged-up and tight-chested. A voice restricted by such cramped conditions will make anyone listening to it feel clogged-up and tight-chested. too.

The upper part of your chest is not, however, a completely redundant space for breath. Think of it as a top-up-tank useful for moments when your thoughts, and therefore your flow of words, run on a bit longer than you had allowed for. At such times you can snatch a quick breath into your upper chest to tide you over until you can take in a fresh deep breath at a sensible stopping point.

To speak audibly over distance and for long periods without tiring, your breath should always be taken at sensible stopping points and drawn from the lower, more capacious area of your chest. To make sure that you can use breath from that area on a regular basis, you need to know how to regulate the rise and fall of your diaphragm.

ABOUT YOUR DIAPHRAGM

Your diaphragm is the dome of muscle fibres which separates your chest from your abdomen and which automatically rises to push breath out of your chest, and lowers to draw air into your chest, every moment of every hour of every day of your life. The edges of that dome are attached to the bottom of your ribs all the way round from your breast bone to your spine.

Between each of your ribs there is a herring-bone lacing of muscle. But only your lower ribs have extensible cartilage points built in to them. You can train the muscles between those extensible lower ribs to fan-out as the diaphragm reaches its point of lowest descent and delay its inevitable rise.

Exercises to help you to do this are simple, but effective.

Sit or stand in a comfortably upright position and count aloud from one to five – one count per second – on one breath.

Count at the same pace from one to eight, on one breath

Gradually extend the count you can speak on one breath.

Go through the same process using lists of names or products.

Use your favourite poems or song lyrics.

Speak one line to a breath, then two lines, then three, and so on.

When you are comfortable with the above, take new breath only when you reach places which make sense of what you are saying.

As a presenter you will need to speak louder than you do in everyday speech and, since the louder you wish to speak the faster your breath has to pulse through your vocal cords, you will need to exert even more control over the muscles which maintain your breath supply.

Raise the volume of your voice and practise your counts and lists and rhymes until you can sustain breaths as comfortably as you did before you increased loudness.

Don't train to become muscle bound, but to have easy access to the muscle power of the rib cage when you want it. But, no matter how expert you become at speaking long phrases on one breath, you should always allow the *sense* of what you are saying to take precedence over the length of phrase you can sustain.

BREATH AND YOUR VOCAL CHORDS

Now that we have thought about the role which the muscles of the ribcage and the dome of your diaphragm play in helping you to sustain the breath you need for speaking in public, we should move our concentration from waist level and take a look at two small folds of muscular tissue, approximately 2.5 centimetres (one inch) long, which lie from front to back inside your neck, behind your Adam's Apple.

Normally, these folds form a valve which either stays open so that you can breathe out and in, or clamps shut so that you can defecate, save yourself from choking or lift heavy objects. But when you decide to speak, a quite remarkable thing occurs.

Breath from your chest rises up your wind-pipe, meets with the valve's muscular folds, and seeks to blow them apart. The impact causes the fold edges (as tough as the Teflon with which they can be repaired should the need arise) to vibrate together and imbue the breath pulsing up between them with sound. The valve edges become vocal cords. Voice begins.

HOW VOICE BEGINS

When the edges of your vocal cords vibrate harmoniously together over breath pulsing regularly between them, they produce clear voice. When the edges of your vocal cords are not so closely in tune, breath pulsing sloppily between them, jostles them into producing breathy voice. When the vibrating edges of your vocal cords are so far apart that breath pulsing between them merely creates friction, they can only produce a whisper.

Place the fingerprint pad of your fore finger very lightly against your Adam's apple.

Make sure that your arm is not resting against your body or any other object.

Say your name and the vibrations of the valve edges lying behind your Adam's apple will cause your finger to vibrate and tingle.

Say your name loudly and you should sense vibrations through the whole of your hand.

Whisper your name. You will sense no vibrations at all.

BREATH AND YOUR VOCAL TRACT

If pulses of breath and the vibrations of the Teflon tough edges of the valve behind the Adam's apple were the sole creators of the human voice, you would only ever make a sound like the one you hear if you blow through a slit in a blade of grass. To become voice as we know it, that squeak must seek extra resonance from inside your vocal tract: the flexible tubular channel running from your vocal cords to the outer edges of your lips. It must rise over your tongue which is anchored behind your Adam's apple and travel through your throat into your pharynx – the cavernous area you see at the back of your mouth when you yawn. It then either surfs behind the muscular drawbridge of your soft palate down your nasal passages and out through your nostrils, or skims over the bulk of your tongue to curve past the hinges of your jaws, between your fleshy cheeks, under the arching hard palate of the roof of your mouth, past your gums and teeth and out through your lips.

To create speech during that journey your pulsating breath will have to be positioned by your tongue to form the vowels and consonants which make up your words.

BREATH, VOWELS & CONSONANTS

Vowel sounds are created when voiced breath pulses over the body of the tongue and is tilted towards resonant surfaces inside the vocal tract's tuneful tube. Vowels form the core of your words; a core which remains in place and taps-in to the resonant spaces of your vocal tract even when you are voiceless.

Whisper the following words one after the other.

"Too, took, toe, taut, top, tar, tusk, terse, tap, ten, tape, tip, team."

Not only will each word be clear, but each vowel placed in that order by your tongue and shaped by your vocal tract will have raised your words semi-tone by semi-tone by one octave.

VOICING VOWELS

Enough of whispering – good presenters need voice and plenty of it to get a message across to an audience. As you work to produce strong core vowels which will resonate in listeners' minds you will discover that the innards of English words have an alarming habit of elongating and changing as you speak them because of tilts of the tongue.

The words, **but**; **them**; **star**; **to**; **rob**; **kill**; **be**; **mat**; **put**; **saw**, look short and have one core sound.

The words, **now**; **high**; **mole**; **few**; **pile**; **boy**; **day**; **hare**; **eel**, look just as short but have two core sounds.

Say all those words yourself and make sure you give their
vowels full value

The short words, **hour**; **pure**; **wire**; **toil**, even have three core sounds when spoken by some English speakers.

Ask the question, "Why?" Elongate and sustain its sound for
as long as you can.

You probably heard yourself saying five vowel sounds: *"ooh, awe, ah, iii, eee,"* and yet that short word is written in consonants.

Vowel sounds sometimes get inserted into spoken English where no vowel exists. A universal example of this is the *"uh"* which appears between the **c** and the **l** in the word **nuclear**. The word is commonly pronounced either as, *noo/**cull**/year* or *"kneeooh/**cull**/yuh."* This is not a crime! Everyone will know what the speaker means. But when you speak in public make sure that you don't unwittingly misplace vowels and so confuse your listeners.

CREATING CONSONANTS
Consonants are the sounds which cause breath to hiss or puff, explode or sizzle as you speak. They are formed when breath is flicked, squeezed or rammed against your palates, teeth and gums by your agile tongue, or frayed at its edges by your vocal cords or as you chew your bottom lip, or pounced on by both lips as the breath tries to escape.

Study the characteristics listed in the box below.

The *bounce* of b and p;	The *twang* of ng;
the *drum-kit brush stroke* of k and t;	the *slap* of l;
the *thud* of d;	the *thrust* of th;
the *chew* of j;	the *glue* of g and y;
the *gnaw* of m and n;	the *thrill* of r;
the *bite* of v and f;	the *wow* of w;
the *haze* of h;	the *shimmer* of s and sh;
the *churn* of ch.	the *buzz* of z.

Use those characteristics as you say the following sentence.

"Skilled speakers choose muscular lip movements, tongue thrusts, taps, trills and tilts to create consonants with which they clarify meaning."
(See also appendix, page 104)

The more clearly you wish to be heard when you speak in public the more strongly you should emphasise consonants because their percussive sounds impinge so easily on the ear. One consonant which you should not emphasise, however, is the glottal stop.

To create this common English consonant, the edges of the vocal cords slam together to abruptly cut off the breath supply, and abruptly cut off sound. If that happens frequently during forceful speech, a hardened patch like a tiny 'corn' eventually appears on the cord edges. As the edges get pitted, they become unable to seat down properly as they vibrate, and so cannot produce clear voice.

Those of you who do not know what a glottal stop feels like should replace each letter *t* with a grunt as you say the following words: *"Mutiny; kettle; water; inter-city; bitterness."* You will then know what it is you are trying to avoid.

USE THE GLOTTAL STOP WITH CAUTION

Those of you who use glottal-stops in your everyday speech may have avoided damaging your vocal cords because your everyday speech is not effortful. But as you speak out more strongly in order to be heard by an audience you will need to cut down the amount of glottal stops you use.

Prolonged use of forceful glottal stops while speaking in public will roughen your voice and diminish its carrying power. You will begin to notice blips which will not go away however much you clear your throat. Left unchecked, your voice will become permanently hoarse. Listen to those actors with native Cockney accents on the popular BBC TV soap, *Eastenders,* to hear evidence of such vocal abuse.

To keep your vocal cords apart and help you to break the habit of using the glottal stop, make a conscious effort to add H's before all the t's in the following sentence.

"Andy's rottweiler ate my pet rabbit."

"HAndy's roHttweiler HaHte my peHt rabbiHt."

You will notice that an H has also been inserted before the words 'Andy' and 'ate'. This is because habitual users of glottal stops plonk one in front of any word which starts with a vowel.

BREATHE LIFE INTO WORDS

Clean vowels and crisp consonants will definitely form clear words but if the voice that delivers them lacks lustre, audiences will choose not to hear them. To discover how puffs of breath can turn a reedy quiver into a vibrant, interesting voice we must follow their journey through throat, nose and mouth into the outside world.

EXPLORE THE SPACE BEHIND YOUR FACE

If you wish to alter the timbre of your voice you have to become aware of how to manoeuvre pulses of breath which leave your vibrating vocal cords into spaces inside your throat, nose and mouth other than those from which you usually draw resonance.

Be realistic. No matter how hard you try, you won't be able to push your voice beyond the limits set by the physical and sexual features you were born with. And your voice will always be less sonorous and sound higher and thinner in the outside world than it does when you hear it through the bones inside your skull.

ESCAPE THE VOCAL DUNGEON
Though your vocal tract can heap resonant riches on the meagre squeak which emerges from your vocal cords, the dank and soggy space which that puny voice first encounters reveals nothing of the treasure in store.

If you keep your voice in a stranglehold at the bottom of your throat, close to the root of your tongue, all you will get is a grunt: as though you have decided to let a genie out of a bottle and stuff him back in again at one and the same time, and he's protesting.

Say *"Uhm"* – the sound you use when you are trying to think of something to say. Hang on to it until you run out of breath.

As your breath diminishes, your voice will begin to sound like a rusty door hinge or a creaking stair.

Use that croaky voice to say your name and address. You will sound as though you have a severe case of laryngitis.

Some presenters value the gravel which throaty resonance adds to their speech; they think it sounds sexy. That may be true. And a tinge of throaty resonance may be fine; but keep your voice floundering in the soggy confines of the bottom of your throat and you will severely limit the amount of volume it can produce and swamp all its vibrancy. What is more, members of any audience will long to clear their throats for you. Indeed, they will feel so uncomfortable that they will pay scant attention to anything you have to say.

FEEL THE PHARYNX

Once sounding breath is able to rise up over the base of your tongue and leave the deepest recesses of your throat, it enters your pharynx: the huge resonance chamber which you see at the back of your mouth as you yawn. This vaulted space is a major source of vocal sonority and can greatly enhance the meagre sound which left your vocal cords.

Open your mouth and jaw **and draw a sharp intake of breath.**

Cold air will strike against the back wall of your mouth marking out a zone from which you can usefully project your words.

Breathe out and swallow a couple of time.

Close your lips firmly **but open your teeth and drop your jaw as low as possible and then breathe in sharply through your nose.**

Again you should feel air strike the back wall of your mouth, though this time it will feel warmer.

Allow your face to become expressionless. **Loosen your lips but keep the back of your mouth and jaw in as open a position as possible.**

Announce your name and address to an imaginary group of twenty listeners. Keep the rear of your mouth as open as possible even when consonant sounds force you to close your lips.

Your face and jaw muscles will feel a bit taut by now, as will the back of your mouth around the tonsil area, and you will probably have yawned quite a lot. Give yourself a break and breathe easily while you listen to your recording.

If you hear a gargling quality, **your voice is being projected from too far down your throat.**

Do the cold zone test again, **and then make sure that your words spout from its very centre.**

The cool, arching sound of an English Cathedral choir boy's voice is created by being largely reliant on the pharynx's vaulted area of resonance. But a speaking voice which relies on it too greatly may sound cold and cause the speaker to seem to be aloof. Nevertheless, if you want a varied, well modulated voice it should always contain elements of resonance from the curved sounding board of the yawning chasm at the back of your vocal tract.

NURTURE NASAL RESONANCE

Behind your soft palate and close to your hard palate is the entrance to the nasal tract which leads to your nostrils.

Whenever you say the consonants **ng**, as in bungling, your tongue has to bunch-up high against the lowering drawbridge of your muscular soft palate to channel sounding breath into your nasal passages.

Discover how your soft palate feels **against your tongue by lingering over the 'ng' common to each of the words below.**

"Hanger; hunger; mongrel; linger; ongoing; singing; belonging; wrongly; jingling; dangling; bungling."

The consonants **m**, as in mother and **n**, as in newts, are also formed by being channelled down your nostrils.

Say the phrases and sentences below. Exaggerate each m and each n sound.

"Kneeling near me. Kneeling near May. Kneeling near Ma. Kneeling near Mo. Kneeling near you."

"My mother's broker mismanaged Miriam's mortgage money."

"Nobody acknowledges Norman's nasty neighbours now."

Listen to the results.

If the voice which emerges sounds sneering and very nasal then your soft palate hasn't allowed sufficient time for the vowel sounds in your words to resonate before the breath carrying those words has been forced down your nose.

Repeat the word *"Gong"* loudly ten times or more.

Drop your jaw as you speak and elongate the vowel.

Then say, "Long gong" ten times or more.

Make sure that the vowel is not being squeezed out by the consonants which surround it.

Try the sentences about Miriam and Norman again. The voice which emerges should now sound more generous as well as cleanly focused.

When you need to compete with a lot of background noise or if your voice is a bit woolly after a throat infection, use the focus of nasality and an easily lowering jaw to help you to project your words.

CONTACT THE HARD PALATE

Voiced breath which has not been deflected down the nasal tract will flow on towards your lips under the percussive arc of the roof of your mouth where its hard palate can lend your voice open, clear tones.

Say, *"cluster, cluster, cluster, cluster, cluster,"*
a few times. Allow the jaw-hinge to drop your mouth open as you make the vowel sounds.

Breath carrying your words will feel as though it is being pressed forward under the bony roof of your mouth and spread from side to side across your tongue. Experiment until you are sure that you can feel that spread taking place.

Visualise your tongue papering the roof of your mouth and forcing excess paste out from the edges of the paper as it gets pressed into place.

Imagine that there is a transparent plastic partition which forces the wave on which your voice is surfing to be funnelled close to the roof of your mouth.

Read those two italicised sentences aloud, **and as the tongue and the bits of the vocal tract are mentioned, make sure that they are doing what the sentences say they are doing.**

Many professional speakers on radio and TV rely greatly on the hard palate to roll out their voices clearly and directly to their audiences. You should rely on it too; though over reliance on its resonance can make you sound cocky and self satisfied.

CHECK THE CHEEKS

As the squeak which left your vocal cords is gaining sonority under the roof of your mouth it is also surging between your cheeks.

Speak with a generous smile which lights up your eyes.

The muscles which raise your cheeks when you smile will lift those sacks of skin and muscle and in so doing, brighten the tone of your voice.

Stop smiling and allow your words to puff out your cheeks as you read on.

Your voice will sound fuller, darker and more rotund.

Whenever your voice sounds thin, plump it up by using chubby-cheeked sound. You will know if you overdo it because you will sound as though you are speaking with a mouth full of hot, new, baby potatoes.

BOUNCE OFF THE GUM RIDGE

The last chance your surfing voice has to alter timbre before it negotiates the barrier reef of your teeth is by gaining resonance from the gum ridge behind your top teeth. To learn how to use this sounding board, you need to do some humming.

To make sure that the humming is really bouncing off the gum ridge's furrowed structure, you need to start with a strongly emphasised letter D. *"DDDummmmmm!"*

If your hum is in the right place it will set the bones buzzing just under your nostrils, cause your top lip to tingle and give your face a sonic massage. Happily, since other people don't think you are too mad if you walk past them humming, this can be practised virtually anywhere.

Say the following words forcefully.

Beeeeeeyyyoootiful (beautiful), Keeeeeeyyyooobic (cubic),

Yyyeeeeeest (yeast), Jeeeeeeyyyooon (June).

**Push particularly strongly with the sides of your tongue against
your upper molars – or the place where those double teeth should be –
as you say the "eeeeeeyyy" part of each word.**

Make sure your lower jaw doesn't lock tight.

Your tongue will ache on both sides when you have articulated those words strongly.
In fact, if your tongue doesn't ache, you haven't pushed forcefully enough.

Try out some text using this powerful, frontal resonator.

Listen to the results.

The gum-ridge is an extremely valuable resonator for public speakers to get to grips
with. Words bouncing off its furrowed prominence so close to the outside world will
ring out with ease and be audible in the largest auditorium or across the bleakest
stadium. In smaller spaces the immediacy of its resonance will allow your voice just
to coast along.

When you speak in *confined* spaces, however, take care not to project your voice from
the ridge too forcefully because doing so will make you sound strident and hectoring.

MOBILISE THE JAW

Situated behind your back teeth on either side of your soft palate, your jaw hinges
control the front opening of your mouth and the volume of space within it. They also
prevent your teeth from forming a barrier to your words.

Place your index fingers one on either side of your cheeks next to your ear holes.

Open your mouth and you will feel two bumps under your touch.

Say your name and address, and those bumps should move down and up as you speak.

As you practise your presentations check regularly to make sure that the bumps alongside your ear holes at the sides of your cheeks are active under your finger tips. They will open-out generous voice to your listeners.

LIMBER UP THE LIPS

Lively lip muscles make such a remarkable difference to the sound and carrying power of a voice that it is difficult to understand why so many people who speak in public seem unaware of their existence. Obviously, they feel their lips at work as they create the consonants **m**, **p**, **b**, **f** and **v**, and may just detect some movement when sounding the letter **w**, but otherwise they speak as though their lips had nothing to do with the job in hand.

Keep your lips firmly closed. Say the following words as distinctly as you can: *"Hey; he, high, hoe, hue."*

By making a great effort you can form vowel sounds without opening your lips as long as your jaw and the rest of your vocal tract are active; but even the keenest listener would be hard put to understand you.

Separate your lips, but keep them motionless. Say the italicised words again as distinctly as you can.

Audience interest might increase if you spoke like that.

Say, *"hay, he, high, hoe, hue,"* one last time, but use your lips to help you.

Yes. It really is worth giving those lip muscles a work out to get your voice to carry out to an audience. They are vital vocal tools.

Flex them into shape as you speak each of the following instructions.

Form your lips into the shape of a letter-box.

Purse your lips together tightly.

Grin and raise your eyebrows.

Flex and tense both lips as you speak.

Keep both lips virtually immobile.

Thrust both lips out in front of your teeth.

Close your lips completely and allow no words to escape.

The last sentence should leave you in no doubt that however strong and vibrant the voice you have created during your exploration of the vocal tract, if you close your lips against it, the sound of that voice will wallow and drown in the backwash of its own breath wave.

DEVELOP YOUR VOCAL CHARACTER

As you tried out the spaces in the vocal tract from which your voice can be projected, you probably found that one of them was much more familiar and easy for you to use than were the others. You may also have noticed, as you listened to yourself, that some of the sounds you made reminded you of speech patterns and sonorities other than your own.

When you were experimenting with the area far back in the mouth and dropping your jaw wide open, you may have noticed that your voice sounded a bit like someone from California, or Northern Ireland. When you were using nasality you may have been reminded of speakers from Liverpool, or felt that you sounded like a character in a Chicago gangster movie. When you were speaking wide and bright from the gum ridge, speakers from Italy or Yorkshire may have come to mind. And when you were trying to use the hard palate as your main focus you may have been surprised to find yourself sounding a bit posh!

From your earliest childhood, the sound of your voice will invariably have been be linked to the speech patterns of your family and to the speech patterns of the peer group with whom you most associated.

Now that you're aware of different voice and speech qualities and how they occur, try to decide which area of the vocal tract you, your family, your partner, your friends and colleagues most often use.

Take note of the vocal similarities, particularly between family members of the same sex.

What facial expressions are there in common between people from the same region?

Is there a body language common to those speakers?

Begin to assess which parts of the vocal tract predominate in the voices of those people.

Turn your attention to common vocal influences from film, television and radio personalities. You will notice that sport's commentators are great examples of athletic articulation. Chat show hosts know how speak easily and put other people at ease. War correspondents are good examples of how to stay cool under pressure.

Listen particularly carefully to the faceless voices used to guide you through TV documentaries. Do they speak matter-of-factly, dramatically, conspiratorially, sadly, or in jocular fashion?

Notice the accent they use, and assess how that, together with their tone of voice, affects you.

Does the way those people speak influence your opinion of them or their subject?

Are you engaged by what you are watching purely because of the voice you hear?

Are you turned-off something you thought you would find fascinating because of the commentary alongside it?

If you find that these matters affect you, pause and consider what you must do so that others are not put off by watching your stance or listening to your way of speaking.

One thing you will be sure to have noticed is that different people speak at different speeds. This is a worry to many who ask for help with voice and presentation. They have been told that because their speech is slow, their speech is lazy. But there is no such thing as lazy speech. Laziness is a concept. Speech, any speech, is a finely honed skill. Individuals have different ways of speaking, that's all. Where some accents require the tongue to be slick, others require it to be sluggish.

As you pay attention to detailed articulation, most of you will find that your speech tends to slow down. This is almost always an advantage to a presentation. But, in case you discover that you are slowing down so much that you sound like a Zombie, make sure that you keep the sense of what you are saying uppermost in your mind. Your brain will then work out a suitable rate of speech to fit your message.

YOUR ACCENT IN PERSPECTIVE

Many clients who ask for help with presentation worriedly ask, **"Does my accent matter?"**. The assumption, even in this Twenty First Century, is that to become a good speaker, a would-be presenter must get rid of a home accent and put a 'better' accent in its place.

In 1922 the British Broadcasting Corporation, the BBC, designated Standard English also known as Received Pronunciation or RP the "correct" accent to be used by anyone who presented on its airways.

In the US, although there was no single arbiter of broadcasting taste, announcers on public radio networks were encouraged to iron out major regional discrepancies and speak with an accent known as Standard American.

For mediums of world wide communication the decisions could be seen to be valid, because each of those accents really does give speech a clarity which is helpful to visitors and immigrants as they struggle to understand and then pronounce the English language.

Even though many presenters on radio and TV in the UK now speak with regional or foreign accents, the BBC's eighty year old edict still exercises enormous influence over people of all ages who assume that when they speak in public they have to use an accent different from their own. Many North Americans who want to be taken seriously as public speakers also believe that they still must rid themselves of their home accent.

Certainly, those of us who wish to speak well in public have to ensure that we can be understood by as many listeners as possible, but that does not mean that it is necessary to learn an accent other than our own. Such specialised training may be necessary for actors who aim to become custodians of the history of spoken language and something other than themselves, but it is not necessary for presenters.

Nevertheless, the 'you' who speaks in public is not likely to be the 'you' who speaks on day to day terms with family, friends or colleagues. It would be wise to ask someone who does not speak with the same accent as you, to listen as you rehearse your presentations and tell you how much they are able to understand. You will then be sure to find the places where what is clear to you, is less so to others.

The answer to the question, *"Does my accent matter?"* is that incomprehensibility is not acceptable in any accent.

GET THE GRAMMAR RIGHT

Incorrect grammar is not acceptable in any accent either. Ungrammatical sentences common to a regional accent have no place in a formal presentation. They stick out of its structure like broken bones and fracture its meaning.

"We was going to town," would be natural as part of a homely, Birmingham, UK, conversation, but it would not be grammatically acceptable to use the singular was to refer to the plural we in a presentation.

There are many such examples of everyday speech habits which would be out of place when speaking in public. If you are unsure of your grasp of this subject, get hold of a copy of a relevant English Grammar and study it well.

> *"My voice is my voice. It's my identity. Take it or leave it.*
> *I'm not going to change it."*

Many of you will sympathise with that gut reaction and feel that your identity is being threatened by suggestions that you should make changes to your voice and your way of speaking. Voice is an intimate part of any person and it is natural to feel vulnerable when discussing its qualities, and attempting change, But what you do when you speak in public is, rather, to *share* your identity, and open it out to a wider audience than it has been able to reach before.

As you pass on interesting information in a generous voice you will enliven even the most listless audience. The surge of energy you receive when that happens will make up for any amount of angst.

CONNECT WITH YOUR BODY

No matter how much you know about the way you can use your vocal tract to re-shape your voice and your accent, if you do not use your body well your voice will lack conviction and your presentation, though it may look strong on the page, will lack impact. Since merely to have to stand in front of an audience is an ordeal for so many presenters, we will attend to feet first.

TAKE A FIRM STAND

Place both feet firmly on the ground with both heels supporting equal weight. Put one foot just slightly in front of the other. Both knees should be loose. Your legs should be a little apart.

With your feet and legs and your shock-absorber knees in this stable position, ensure that your crotch, the middle of your pelvis, is always under the centre of the trunk of your body.

Allow your flexible spine to keep your back straight.

Make sure that the middle of the crown of your skull is always in direct alignment with the centre of the trunk of your body.

Stand for a while in this relaxed, upright stance, then, keeping your head and back upright, drop directly into a crouch.

Your knee joints will probably crack, but if you don't topple sideways or to the front or to the back, you will have found the correct posture.

Once you've got your upright stance balanced correctly, you will be able to drop to an upright crouch over and over again – and once your knees get used to folding, they will probably remain silent.

From such a well-grounded, upright position, you will be able deliver your message in a strong and interesting voice. You will feel secure. You will look secure, and you will communicate a sense of security to your audience.

Should you choose or need to sit to give your presentations make sure you sit upright so that your body weight doesn't rest over the base of your spine and inhibit its natural flexibility. Make sure that your rib-cage isn't squashed, your shoulders aren't hunched and your head isn't hanging down. Sit, as you stood: upright and centred over the middle of your pelvis.

MOVE PURPOSEFULLY

There is no reason to stay rooted to the spot when you talk in public, but moving about should never distract you from the meaning of your words.

Watch footballers whilst they are running and kicking. Watch tennis players whilst they are playing a running, backhand shot. Watch hurdlers as they cross each barrier. Despite all the effort those athletes are expending, their bodies remain balanced. No matter how heated the activity, each player's concentration is directed towards finding the best position to drive the body or the ball to the place where it can be most effective. The most uninformed onlooker is able to tell when an athlete loses concentration. The most inattentive audience member will notice when a presenter has lost the plot.

ASK FOR FEED BACK

Ask someone to watch you and listen to you as you move about. Ask them to give you feedback.

Get someone to video you as you walk about, then you can give yourself feedback.

Make sure that you are not always walking at the same pace or to the same place.

Make sure that all of your listeners can see you all of the time.

Make sure that bodily movement does not shake your voice.

Walk lightly. Don't plonk your heels down and distract from what you are saying with noisy footfalls. Two feet on an uncarpeted floor can sound like a herd of elephants.

Keep your mind on the sense of what you are saying.

Think evenly and allow the breath which carries your words to stream out of your mouth at the same even pace as the flow of your thought.

CONTROL THE MOVEMENT OF YOUR UPPER LIMBS

Arm yourself against allowing your hands and arms to give out signals that counteract your message.

"Concentrate on my next point because it is the key to the whole argument," says your voice, whilst your hands flutter aimlessly, and diminish your words.

"And here is the nub of the matter." you say, as your hand reaches into a pocket.

Listeners will naturally assume that the main point of your argument is in that pocket, and you will wonder why there is laughter at such an inappropriate moment.

WATCH OUT FOR YOUR HANDS AND ARMS

Practise your presentation in front of a long mirror or a video camera. Make sure that the mirror or the camera is angled so that, from feet to fingertips, you are visible in the frame.

There will probably be so many things happening to your arms and hands without your being aware of them that you'll wonder whether you have been possessed by gremlins.

a) While you are concentrating on keeping your hands still, are your elbows doing the funky-chicken and twitching out and in?

> ## Your material is probably too dense for the time allowed and your elbows are clutching at you to spur you on.
>
> **Slow down the pace of your speaking until the twitching stops.**
> **If necessary leave some material out!**

b) Are your hands moving freely but your elbows looking as if they have been taped to your sides?

> ## Release the arm lock you are putting on yourself.
>
> **Release the breath you were holding, too.**

c) Does your right hand become a closed fist while your left hand gestures in an open and friendly manner, or vice versa?

> ## Choose which signal you are trying to convey.
> **Use it to good effect.**

d) Are those ten little devils (commonly called fingers) fiddling and twitching without you being aware of them? What are the two most intractable of the evil crew, the thumbs, up to?

> ## Shake your arms and hands vigorously then give your digits something to do which fits your words – and see that they do it.

e) Are you trying to keep your upper limbs under control by hanging on to a lectern or a clip-board, papers or a pen with so much tension that it travels up through your hands and arms, tightens your chest and strangles your voice?

> ## Squeeze your whole body into as tight a ball as you possibly can and then consciously release that tension.
>
> **Each time you become aware of tension building take a firm grip on it. Squeeze it – and then release it by shaking it out of your system.**

Concentrate on the meaning you are trying to convey, and you will automatically control your limbs. Even when you are speaking from a prepared text or have memorised a planned script, speak as though you are creating fresh ideas moment by moment. As you concentrate on making sense of what you are saying your body will tune-in to this creative thought process and even its extremities will become visibly more comfortable. Every part of you will become intent on making sure that you get your message across.

HOLD YOUR NECK UP

We human beings are marked out from other animals by the way we function on two legs in an upright position, and yet we insist on using our necks as though we were four legged racehorses. Because the neck is very flexible, we expect it to support the weight of the head without any help from the strong-boned yoke of the shoulders, and then we complain of neck-ache! The poor old neck designed to allow the head to tilt and turn whilst always keeping it centred over the top of the rest of the spine, is left to dangle the brain's great weight with no help from any front legs or any weight-bearing bone.

Your vocal cords lie inside your neck, directly behind the Adam's apple, so they take quite a battering when you hang your head without the underpinning of your body's frame. Imagine being in a lift if the lift shaft kept undulating. You'd be thrown from side to side and up and down. Even with protective panels, a trampoline for a floor and no ceiling, you'd eventually feel sore and weak and near to collapse – yet that is the sort of strain we regularly put our vocal cords under in the lift shaft of our necks. No wonder voices get tired and sound worn as we force them to function under such conditions. When you hang your head forward, or squash it down or allow it to loll from side to side, your neck has no alternative but to call on the strength of a multiplicity of muscles which were designed to keep far distant areas of your body in shape. Is it any wonder that you begin to ache in all kinds of seemingly unrelated places?

PROTECT YOUR VOICE FROM 'GETTING IT IN THE NECK'

Never again twist, **turn or lean your neck unless your feet, your knees, your pelvis, your hips or your shoulders have instigated and are underpinning that movement.**

Make sure that the centre of the crown of your head is always over the centre of the yoke of your shoulders. The bone structure at the back of your neck – the part behind your ears – can then stay poised over the rest of your flexible spine and be supported by your shoulder girdle.

Never again jut-out your chin and pull your vocal cords out of alignment to emphasise a point. Tilt your forehead towards your audience for emphasis, instead.

Your shoulder girdle acts as a rolled-steel-joist (RSJ). It is the T-Frame which bears the weight of your body's upper-storey which houses your precious and heavy brain.

PUT YOUR BACK INTO WHAT YOU ARE DOING

Strong voice requires support from a fully rounded person. This means that you should pay as much attention to the back of your body as you do to its front. If you ignore your back you become spineless. You half-starve your lungs. You become half-hearted and unable to put your back into the energetic exercise required for powerful communication.

Stand upright and centred over your pelvis; legs slightly apart, knees loose, head balanced over the centre of the yoke of your shoulders, arms hanging loose.

Imagine that someone has placed a bar-stool under your buttocks as you stand there.

Keep your body posture as it is, and just make the small adjustment you would need to ledge your bottom on the imaginary stool.

Try out that 'ledging' movement – that 'little sit' – a couple of times and pay particular attention to what happens to the upper part of your back under your shoulder blades – the part of your back that is level with your armpits.

There will not be a very noticeable movement, but you will probably be aware that this distinctive 'ledging' posture has widened your upper back slightly.

This small but very significant postural alteration frees up the lower part of your rib cage and opens out a more capacious area from which to power the extra breath you need in order to speak strongly without tiring.

Watch videos of the Three Tenors. All of them, but particularly Placido Domingo, take a 'little sit' as they power-out their top notes. They know that to make full bodied sound they must put their backs into it.

Imagine that you have to lift an extremely heavy box which your arms can only just encompass.

Keep your head upright. Keep the back of your neck centred over your shoulder girdle to give your head firm support and crouch down to lift that box.

Allow your feet, knees and strong leg muscles to take the strain.

Lift your heavy box like Olympic weight-lifters do until you reach a balanced standing position.

Hold on to the weight for a few seconds.

The widening sensation at the top of your back under your shoulder blades will feel really obvious to you now.

OK. Just drop the box. It is, after all, only an imaginary thing.

All of the exercises suggested here will train the muscles needed to lend your voice firm support. Strong thigh muscles and flexed knees will bear the weight of your torso. Strong back muscles will hold your torso firmly but not fixedly, upright. A strong shoulder girdle will support the weight of your head on its flexible but upright neck. You will discover that by supporting your bodyweight in this way you are able to speak-out without tiring, for a considerable length of time.

There is an unexpected bonus to the upright, balanced posture you need to expand vocal control: your body will appear leaner and fitter, and your vitality will be enhanced. There is an unexpected bonus when you use well articulated, energetic speech: your eyes will appear brighter, your cheek, jaw and neck muscles taut and youthful. You get a body-tone and a face lift rolled into one.

MODULATE YOUR PITCH

As long as your body gives your voice balanced support, normal, healthy vocal cords will alter pitch of their own accord time and time again. But, if your posture is tugging in opposing directions, the vocal cords and their assistant muscles have a struggle to maintain a correct balance. Too much movement of your ribcage, too much waggling of your neck and head as you speak will cause your voice to strain and crack and will eventually lead to muscle fatigue and voice loss.

Take a thick elastic band. Put it round a chair leg or a door handle.

Pull the band taut with one hand, pluck it with the fingers of the other hand, and you will hear a fairly high pitched twang.

Allow the elastic to be a little less taut, and pluck it again. This time the twang will sound somewhat lower.

The tauter the band: the higher the pitch of the note.

The slacker the band: the lower the pitch of the note.

PITCH AND POSTURE

The elastic tissue and muscle of your vocal cords, which lie from front to back across the bottom of your throat, need to be shorter and slacker for low pitches, longer and tauter for high pitches.

Do not lead with your chin or stretch your neck and thrust your Adam's apple out of alignment when you are speaking emphatically, but lower your forehead and nudge or head butt your audience into taking notice of you. Your horizontal vocal cords will then remain slung at ease behind your Adam's apple and be able to concentrate on the flexing and tensing needed to serve you well.

MARK YOUR PITCH

No matter what pitch your voice is aiming for as it leaves the horizontal, vibrating vocal cords behind your Adam's apple, it has to have an outlet.

Look at your face, neck and shoulders in a mirror.

Draw a line with shaving foam or make-up across that mirror image to indicate the level from which you think low-pitched voice should come.

Draw a similar line to indicate the level from which high pitched voice should come.

Where did you draw those lines?

The first should stretch across your face from one earlobe to the other, so that it passes immediately under your cheek bones and nostrils.

That's the place from which to produce even your lowest pitch.

The second line should run across your forehead, from the top of one ear to the top of the other ear, following the level of your eyebrows.

That's the place from which to produce even your highest spoken pitch.

Your voice can only be sounded from inside your vocal tract. Since there are no holes in either the front or back of your chest or the front or back of your neck, it has to travel over your tongue, up your throat, under your cheek bones, down your nose and through your mouth on a boomerang curve, to get to the outside world.

Admittedly, when you raise and lower pitch as you speak out strongly, you will be aware of sensations inside your body. At higher pitches, most of the reverberations will be absorbed by the bony structure of the skull. But at lower pitches you may feel reverberations in your face, breast bone and upper back. Do not be fooled into thinking that the stronger the bodily reverberations you feel, the better your voice will sound in the outside world. Learn to rely more on sensations which occur behind your face and inside your head as you speak.

PITCH HIGHER

Say "Hmm," in the way you usually do when agreeing with someone.

Turn that spoken "Hmm," into a prolonged, intoned hum and then pitch it a semi-tone higher.

Maintain the higher pitch, and turn the hum back into the "Hmm," of spoken agreement.

Maintain that new pitch while you record some of your presentation.

Using this method, raise your pitch – one semitone at a time – by three or four steps.

Practise and record your chosen text at each level.

PITCH LOWER

Say "Hmm," in the way you usually do when agreeing with someone.

Turn the spoken "Hmm" into a prolonged, intoned hum and then pitch it a semi-tone lower.

Turn that lower pitched hum back into the "Hmm" of spoken agreement.

Practise your presentation in the new lower voice you will have acquired.

Begin again. Lower your pitch – one step at a time – by three or four steps.

Practise your chosen text at each step. Record yourself as you do so.

Allow the recording to suggest the optimum pitch for your voice, and once you have found that pitch use it whenever you speak in public. Ideally, use it all the time.

PITCH PRACTISE

Try out a few dummy runs of a genuine presentation placing your voice at both higher and lower pitches than you would usually use.

Ask friends or colleagues to tell you which pitch they think suits you best – which pitch sounds most comfortable to them. Accept the advice you are given.

Believe your listeners' ears rather than your own, especially as the listeners will often select a pitch which is higher than you would have chosen for yourself.

If your voice is pitched too low as you practise, it will creak.

If your voice is pitched too high as you practise, it will squeak.

In either case, you will probably be aware of a physical click just behind your Adam's apple. The click indicates that your vocal muscles need further practise in order to take on their new task smoothly.

You may also have felt a tickle low down in your throat which made you cough. This suggests that you were not allowing breath to flow evenly through your vocal cords as you spoke. The escalator of breath must always be moving when a voice begins its journey to an audience.

PRACTISE YOUR SCALES

Travellers queuing to buy rail tickets at a busy London station are directed to ticket desks numbered one to eight by a recorded announcement. The pitch range of the announcement by both a male and a female voice follows exactly the same contours.

*"Cashier number **eight**, please,"*

The range of the sentence covers a whole octave with the word *eight* sounding exactly one octave above the first syllable *Cash*.

Cash/ier/num/ber/***eight***/please.

Do / re/ mi/ fa/ ***do*** /   re

A good quality speaking voice should regularly cover two octaves to maintain the attention and interest of listeners.

INCREASE YOUR PITCH RANGE

If your vocal cords are to range easily up and down octaves, they must be kept actively involved in making pitch changes.

Start on as low a note as is comfortable for you, and make the sound *"shoo."*

Swoop your voice as high as you can and, without pausing, swoop back down to the note you started on.

Repeat this exercise five or six times.

Use the same starting note and test yourself to see if you can reach a higher peak.

Keep returning to the same base note, but aim higher and higher.

Stop only when you feel you've exhausted that possibility.

Make sure that when you have reached a new high plateau, you go over the swoop five or six times before you try to climb to the next plateau.

If you were disappointed with the results you were getting from those exercises and thought your voice just wasn't reaching high enough, try again, but this time use visualisation to help you.

Imagine a range of mountains with peaks of varied heights. You are in a valley one side and your voice has got to reach people standing in a valley on the other side of the mountains.

Start by imagining that you are standing fairly high up on the sides of your valley and swoop your voice over the lowest peak of the range to someone who is equivalently placed in the opposite valley.

Extend your range by imagining yourselves standing lower and lower in the valley sending the *"shoo"* sound over ever higher peaks to a person moving lower and lower down the sides of their valley.

You have aimed for the sky, now plumb the depths.

Practise in the same manner as for the ascending swoops, but this time imagine that the *"shoos"* are life lines being plunged down into a subterranean cave where you and a group of pot-holers are trapped at increasingly lower levels.

You will be surprised how low your vital voice can plunge even at your first attempt when it is a matter of life or death.

Try out these extraordinary swoops while driving your car – though it's a bit cruel to try them out when you've got passengers. Get out onto beaches or into parks and other open spaces and shoo to your heart's content. Zap out two or three shoos quite loudly when walking along a busy street or as a train arrives on a station platform – there is so much noise at those moments that nobody will hear you at all. In any case, these days, people will ignore whatever sound you choose to make as you walk down the street. They will assume you are on your cell phone, whereas you will be discovering that opening uninhibited voice to the world invigorates all the cells in your body.

CREATE INTEREST WITH PITCH CHANGES

If a presenter's voice is stuck on a monotone, captive audience members feel as though they are stuck on a train just outside its destination. They long to get off and onto the platform in sight, but they can't. Conversely, when a presenter alters pitch too often, audiences feel as though they are stuck on a roller-coaster.

By far the best way to tackle the journey of a presentation is to walk with listeners up and down gentle inclines and climb shallow steps with them. Everyone can keep pace with you and follow your considered footsteps. An occasional jolt when you hoist them to a dizzy height or reveal an unexpectedly deep chasm will then have a memorable impact.

FIND THE BEST PITCH LEVEL

Cultural attitudes and peer group pressure may make it difficult for you to agree to make pitch alterations to your voice even though habitual speech patterns may be undermining your ability to deliver effective presentations. Be brave. Be prepared to stand out from the crowd. That's what presenters do.

Certain men value 'growl' in a voice, because they think it sounds macho. They feel threatened when it is suggested that a higher pitch may make speaking in public easier, and cannot accept that such a change would make them sound more pleasing to an audience.

Some female presenters, asked to try speaking at a lower pitch, feel that to do so will undermine their femininity or make them sound domineering.

Some non-native speakers expected to deliver presentations in English, find it difficult to let go of pitches appropriate to their native languages and feel inhibited when asked to do so.

All of the above are valid personal concerns, but presenters planning presentation pitches should most concern themselves with ensuring that audiences are able to understand what is being said.

VARY YOUR VOLUME

We all encounter people speaking on their mobile phones who seem unaware how clearly their conversation is carrying to others around them. Those of us at the far end of a railway carriage, or a long way down the same street, are forced to listen because the speakers are so distinctly audible. Extraneous noise on the train or in the street or on their phone line means that the person on the phone is listening extra hard to make out what is being said. When people can't hear well they assume that they can't be heard well, and so they speak up. Use their example. Practise your presentation as though you were on a cell phone in a noisy place. Then, even if you turn your back on your audience, you will be sure to be heard.

GET YOUR VOICE OUT OF YOUR MOUTH

If you were walking about and talking deep inside a huge loud-hailer, your words would not carry to those waiting outside to hear you unless you made your way to the hailer's outer rim. Many of us keep our voices deep-down inside our throats, deep inside our own loud-hailers, and then wonder why making ourselves heard is such a strain. Hoist your voice to the front of your mouth. Get it to the rim of your loud hailer. You will be amazed at the difference which so simple an idea can make to the carrying power of your words. To find out how to do that hoist, let's simulate a voice that is locked inside the funnel of a loud-hailer.

Close your lips firmly and clench your teeth together. Say: "Hey, you out there, are you listening to me? I intend to be clearly heard."

That was difficult to say, never mind hear, wasn't it?

Now, open your lips but keep the teeth together. Repeat: "Hey, you out there, are you listening to me? I intend to be clearly heard."

Notice how much easier it was to create the words you were speaking, that time. Any listener would tell you how much more clearly the speech could be heard.

This time, allow your teeth and lips to move as they usually do but hold your nostrils tight shut.

Say again: *"Hey you out there, are you listening to me? I intend to be clearly heard."*

Notice how constrained you feel at the back of your mouth when you say, "listening to me" and "intend." In fact, you probably feel constricted on all of, "intend to be clearly heard."

So, now, speak the sentences in the same way, still holding your nostrils tight shut, but open your mouth exaggeratedly wide as you speak.

Notice that the feeling at the back of the mouth on the *"n"* and the *"ng"* didn't feel half as clogged as it did when you first squeezed your nostrils together.

Finally, allow your mouth and nostrils to be free but cup your hands in front of them.

Speak the sentences again. *"Hey, you out there, are you listening to me? I intend to be clearly heard."*

Try again, and uncup your hands at the 'karate chop' edges from time to time as you do so. Carry on speaking about any topic while using this 'karate chop' opening and closing method.

Observe that a wider opening allows for more volume. Observe that a specific focus allows for more volume.

Put your forefingers on your cheeks right next to the centre
of your ear holes and open your mouth wide.

Two bumps will appear under your fingers.

Say your name and address and those two bumps will move up and
down under your touch.

This exercise is so important it is worth repeating here because audibility will
increase significantly if you allow your jaw hinges to drop your mouth open in a
more pronounced way than when you are chatting with friends.

CHOOSE A POINT OF VIEW?

To find a view point will also help your audiences to listen to your point of view.
Most of us have places in our own homes from where we can see for a distance.
We can look out of a window at the sky or at a far off chimney. Even if we live in a
space with no windows, most of us have a mirror somewhere.

Place a mirror against a wall or lean it on a chair or on a
table, and take up a position as far away from it as you can. This will
give the sense of twice as much distance as there is in the room.

Three metres or nine feet instantly becomes six metres or eighteen feet.

Direct what you have to say towards some object at eye level and at the
furthest possible distance from yourself. (It need only be a dirty mark on
your wall or a leaf on a branch.)

Talk to that object. Concentrate on the distance that your words must
cover to get to it.

Tell the object or mark what you have to say. *Intend* that your message
will reach it and your message *will* reach it.

You will not get a response from the inanimate objects you have chosen to speak to. Some live groups you address when you give a presentation will be equally inert! Do not despair. Though you are responsible for your message and the way in which you deliver it, you are not responsible for the way in which individuals choose to receive it.

ADD TO YOUR VOCAL RANGE

You now know how to stop yourself becoming clogged up with breath and how to stop your voice from sounding constricted. You now know how to ensure that the air inside you does not become stale and slow up your thinking. You now know how to make yourself heard. Take responsibility for all that knowledge as you follow the next steps.

Choose a newspaper article that interests you.

Prepare your posture for presentation. Breathe out.

Allow your diaphragm to draw fresh air deep into your lungs.

Allow that air to start to flow out again, and begin to read aloud for as long as your breath will allow you.

If your voice tails off before you've got to the place you intended to get to, try again; but this time concentrate on the *sense* of the words you are saying.

You are likely to find that you can get through the phrase the second time with a surprising amount of breath to spare. If you are still unsuccessful: breathe out fully, and try once more.

If you still didn't quite make it, work out the exact point at which your breath started to fail. It may well be that the sensible stopping point you aimed for the first time was not so sensible for you.

Choose other reading matter and repeat these ideas, until allowing your breath to make sense for you as you speak out is no longer a matter of conscious effort.

Aim to tell a person who is half-way across a football pitch something which you need to say and they need to hear.

Don't shout, but intend to be heard.

Open up your jaw hinges.

Emphasise key words to project your meaning.

Let words spin from your mouth and arc towards their target audience. Aim to make your words hit the ground just in front of your imaginary listener's feet.

The following exercise will help you to be somewhat aware of how you sound to other people who listen to you.

Start to read out loud, and then cup a hand over one ear.

Notice the difference in the resonance you hear – quite nice isn't it? – Quite flattering.

Now cup both hands over both ears.

Practise reading aloud like that for a few minutes, then snatch your hands away whilst you continue speaking

You may be a bit disappointed this time as the voice you hear probably sounds more thin and diffuse than you had expected it to sound. Nevertheless, keep going without cutting down the volume.

Get used to that thinner sound. It is your voice out in the open.

Cup your hands over both ears and speak or read aloud.

Keep speaking and uncover your ears.

Hold your hands over both ears once more as you speak, and again, after a little while, uncover your ears.

Each time you uncover your ears, the volume of your voice may surprise you. It may not be as loud as you thought it was going to be. If that is the case, keep your hands away from your ears and increase loudness until you reach the volume you *assumed* you were making when your hands were cupped over your ears.

Continue to speak at that new higher volume, then, cup your hands over your ears once more.

The loudness of the voice which greets you now, will probably be too much for you to enjoy with your ears covered in this way. You will probably be aware of uncomfortable pressure in your ears. Nevertheless, carry on speaking at that volume for a moment or two before you take your hands from your ears whilst still speaking.

If you feel as though you are now shouting, keep going at that same volume, but say your words in a sexy, enticing or gentle way.

The outcome is often very amusing. Laugh at yourself, but keep going, as this method will add variety and warmth to your tone of voice even at very loud volume.

NEVER SHOUT

Shouting positively prevents understanding. When people are being shouted at they feel as though they are being buffeted by a strong wind which, if you think about it, is exactly what is happening to them. If you shout you will wear out the most willing listeners.

Even if you *intend* to harangue or brow beat an audience, there is still no need to shout. Just say your words in a derogatory, harsh or brutal way, and that will do a forceful job for you.

BEAM AT YOUR AUDIENCE

Stand in front of a long mirror. Imagine yourself with one large eye in the middle of your forehead.

Focus that imaginary eye on your imaginary audience as though it were a searchlight beam.

Begin to speak out loud. Project your words along the beam.

Keep your real eyes on your image in the mirror as you do this and you will notice that your forehead tilts down a little.

Shape-up like a boxer who's aim is always to protect, never to project, the chin.

You can now choose either literally to brow beat your audience into sitting up and taking notice of you, or to deliver your message to them with a benign nod. In either case your posture will help your voice to present and sustain a focused argument.

Learn from these methods that you can sound gentle at greater volume than you are used to using, and that you can also sound forceful at lesser volume than you might have thought you would need to use. Your voice can be cajoling, dominating, reassuring, persuasive or downright nasty. Speak in a quietly menacing tone as you practise, and you'll discover just how true that last point is.

FOCUS, RIGHT BETWEEN THE EYES

There is one other area which may prove useful as you learn how to project resonant voice. Inside your face, between your eyes, there is a network of cavities and bony tracery. Some voice specialists feel that there is nothing to be gained from this sinus network because it is so damped by its covering of mucous membrane. But, think how distinctive the voice of a person speaking with a cold in the head sounds. Think about how your own voice sounds to you when you have a cold. It seems far more rich and sonorous than when your sinuses are clear.

Recall the echoing sensations from above and around the bridge of the nose which you are aware of inside your head when you have a cold.

Try to mimic those sensations as you speak. Record your efforts.

You may find that you hear a warmer, more rounded quality in your voice than you have done before, and that your voice sounds more immediate.

If this is the case and the cold in the head idea is helpful to you; use it.

LET YOUR VOICE SPEAK FOR YOU

As you have tried out all the above exercises you will have heard differences in vocal quality and volume. Be assured, that if your voice has sounded louder to you it will definitely sound louder to your audience. You are as close to your voice as it is possible to get and much too close to assess the impact of your voice on others, but if you *intend* to be heard your brain will automatically provide the volume control for your voice's inherent sense of direction.

Once the muscles which activate your voice have been given a chance to learn how to adjust to effort which they have never before experienced, they will take on their task automatically. Your task is to get used to the sensations inside your face and your head which speaking at higher volume creates so that you can automatically summon up just such a volume-adjusted voice whenever you have to speak in public.

Any time you think that you may be losing easy access to good quality, powerful voice use the ideas suggested above. Speak aloud about any subject you care to think of.

Read from cigarette or soap-powder packets. Read from sauce or wine bottles. Read from the lightest magazine, or from the weightiest tome. Recall nursery rhymes, poems, or song lyrics. Just keep on speaking with your new found openness. By doing this you will give your musculature the chance to retain vocal variety and range.

Muscles learn surprisingly fast. Your voice will soon be able to tune-in to speaking at louder volume without your having to go through so rigorous a process, and you will become used to your expansive voice.

TAKE YOUR TIME

Don't try to rush the process of change. Allow yourself to take the time that you need to allow new habits to take hold. Practise fruitfully. Check your posture from time to time. Work on a variety of texts. Listen to yourself to make sure that don't sound harsh and false, but clear and true.

It will become easier and easier for you to create volume and to assess the impact of that volume. You will soon be able to fine-tune your voice to reach small and close or large and distant groups of listeners at will. What is more, such animated speaking will give both you and your listeners quite a buzz!

CARE FOR YOUR VOICE

■ If you have to eat a meal just before a presentation, ensure that you don't eat or drink too much as this can have a clogging and drying effect on the voice; not to mention the clogging effect it can have on the mind!

■ An over-full stomach will hamper control over the flow of your words. If there is too much stuff wandering about in your gut, your diaphragm simply can't push down as low as it should to draw-in the reserves of breath you need.

■ Chocolate, cream and cheese all produce extra mucus and are likely to cause you to clear your throat and swallow more than you normally do. Bits of nut may attach to the sides of your throat and shift when you start to speak and cause you to cough.

■ Your throat may be dry before a presentation, so drink any liquid, warm or cold that does not contain alcohol. This is not to suggest that you should become a teetotaller in order to give presentations, it is simply that alcohol acts as a drying agent, and will automatically aggravate the very symptom you are trying to relieve.

■ Even though you are a non-smoker, other people's cigarette smoke will dry your throat. If the atmosphere is smoky, breathe out and then breathe in through your nose before you begin to speak. Allow the nostrils to filter and humidify air you take in; that is what they were designed for.

■ If your mouth is dry before you speak – and if you are nervous it will be – rub the underside of your tongue gently over your bottom teeth or suck the tip of your tongue a little to stimulate the saliva glands.

■ If there is time, take a drink of something hot or cold, suck a sweet or an ice cube a few moments before you are due to begin. All of these will activate your saliva glands.

■ Never be tempted to have something in your mouth as you speak. Nervousness makes us all want to swallow more than is normal so there is a danger that you may choke on the very thing which was supposed to be helping your voice to feel more free.

■ You are likely to find that your throat aches after your presentation. That's to be expected. You will have been speaking louder and for longer than usual. When they have to do unusual exercise, muscles always let you know about it afterwards.

■ If you have had a long haul flight to a venue, your vocal cords – like your ankles – will become swollen. To avoid huskiness, it would be wise to drink extra water during your flight and after you arrive at your destination.

■ Organise your travel arrangements if at all possible to allow a few hours without much chat after you've landed, and before you have to give your presentation. Give your vocal cords time to readjust.

■ Prolonged shouting damages the edges of the vocal cords, so do your best to avoid shouting for your favourite team at a match, or yelling over loud music at parties before you have to speak in public. Scream only in the direst emergency.

■ If you have to wear spectacles or bifocal lenses, and you have not been used to doing so, you will have to alter the tilt of your head in order to look first at the page then at the audience. Modify the whole of your posture so that you do not have to raise your chin and stretch your neck and compromise the ability of your vocal cords to work freely.

- If you lose teeth or have dentures fitted, your ability to articulate will be changed and you will have to work out with your tongue how to accommodate to this new situation.

- If you have tonsils removed, your voice is likely to sound and feel quite different because of the new space opened up at the back of your mouth and you will have to get used to those new sensations

- Your speech may sound slurred if your tongue is swollen after dental treatment.

- Every time you work on damaged cords you undermine their ability to recover peak condition.

- Seek professional help if any one of the following warning signs is present: your throat feels sore or is clogged with mucus; your sinuses are blocked; your voice appears intermittently or sounds hoarse; your voice is a lot deeper than usual.

- If you have to doctor yourself, try neither to talk nor to whisper for a few hours. Drink lots of liquid both hot and cold. Inhale steam into your mouth and nostrils. Use only those pain-killers designed to ease sore throats: aspirin can cause bleeding when vocal cords are swollen.

- The finest voice when unwell can sound embarrassingly awful, and listeners become so concerned that they are unable to take in what is being said. Realise that sometimes you have to get someone else to speak for you so that your voice lives to tell the tale another day.

PART 2

YOU AND
YOUR PRESENTATION

You are on your way to present your ideas to people you have not met before but whose reputation is impressive. You know it would add to your status and advance your career if, in turn, you could impress them. You take care about your appearance. You check your route and how long the journey is likely to take. You allow extra time for possible delays; it will be better for you to arrive in the vicinity of the meeting place far too early than to be even a couple of minutes late. You have papers related to the presentation you have been asked to make checked out, and in your briefcase. You have prepared this presentation on your lap-top, on a carousel of slides, on overheads, and as a script, so that you will not be thrown into confusion should there be no projector available, or, a sudden power cut occurs. You have spoken your presentation many, many times to the bathroom mirror, to the cat, to your partner, to the lamp post across the street and you know that it fits into the time allowed. If you drive yourself to the venue you have the opportunity to try out what you have planned to say in as loud a voice as you like and as many times as the length of the journey will allow. If you travel on public transport, you have time to go over your speech meticulously in your mind; yet, despite all your careful preparation you feel flustered, uncomfortable, lacking in concentration and altogether unnerved.

You need an instant fix.

Instead of using the journey time to go over the same ground that you have been covering for days, give yourself a break.

USE VISUALISATION

Just as the New Zealand All Blacks take on warrior personae before their games both to 'psyche themselves up' and to inhibit their opponents, visualise yourself into a situation which will gear you up to take on the stressful event and inhibit any thought of failure.

Imagine yourself delivering the presentation you have so carefully prepared, and doing it brilliantly.

Picture yourself feeling really good about the job you have done.

Picture yourself being feted afterwards over a really fine meal and being given the coveted contract or the desired acclaim.

That exercise will be particularly helpful to you if you are unwell or lack lustre for any reason, since a dearth of adrenalin on such occasions can be as destructive to a presentation as an excess of it.

The most common cause of nervous distress before a presentation is, however, too much adrenalin sloshing about the body. If this is your experience, take heart from the fact that even the most polished and urbane speakers experience the fast heart beat, the breathlessness and the queasy stomach which pre-performance nerves can induce. Indeed some find themselves so unnerved that they feel as though they have flu a day or so before they have to get up to speak, or are literally sick a few moments before hand.

In order to get the nerve to build your ego rather than allow nerves to demolish it, you would do best to put all thoughts of the imminent presentation behind you and allow yourself to concentrate on a calming image.

Travel in your mind's eye to places that you know where you
always feel safe and happy.

Sit by a lake or by the sea, or in a garden. Be with your favourite
person. Stroke your cat or your dog. Soak in a bath. Climb mountains or
dive into oceans. Go sailing or surfing.

Keep filling your mind's eye with feel-good factors until you reach your
destination.

Once there, snap energetically back to the job in hand.

As long as your presentation or speech has been well prepared, you will be surprised
to find what a boost to your confidence relaxing beforehand in this way can be.
Realise that if you are too 'keyed up' before a speech or presentation or lecture,
you may squander any well thought out strategy and 'blow the whole thing.'

Take your pulse before and after these momentary visualisations
and feel for yourself how readily your body responds to the influence of
visualisation.

SEARCH THE MIND'S EYE

Emotion attached to recollected events is not only of value before you speak, but
also during your presentation and after you have finished. Whether your subject is
scientific, mathematical, managerial, or of a philosophical or historic nature, it
should always contain verbal illustrations to amplify the ideas you wish to share
with an audience.

The search for such imagery does not need to be made during long hours in
libraries or on the internet. You have stacks of stereoscopic images in your own
mind which the lenses of your eyes have been taking-in over years. And since you
are not merely a camera, images which you develop from the store in your mind

involve other senses too. Make use of images with which you are involved, so that listeners are drawn to remember what you say.

Many presenters feel ill at ease using metaphor, simile and analogy to explain ideas. They see such devices as frippery which sullies their clean, succinct descriptions. In the desire to appear hard-nosed, business-like and professional they ignore the fact that the first task facing any presenter is to stimulate audience imagination. Algorithms, equations or theories of management are stories to be told, just as are tales of historical discovery, medical case history or legal defence. Differences may occur in the terminology common to each discipline, but the main task for any presenter is to unfold a story for an audience and help listeners to absorb what is being said.

Great orators throughout time and from all disciplines and cultures have used imagery to persuade people to their points of view. Draw on their example. Choose the photographic reproduction of simile or the impressionistic quality of metaphor – it doesn't matter which; just use them. They are the slides and overheads of your spoken words.

CONCENTRATE ON VIVID RECALL

When we recollect experiences from the past or plan future scenarios we take for granted the power the brain has to compress time. A lecture or speech which may in real time have taken an hour can be reviewed in seconds; its style, its audience and its venue can be revisited with pleasure (or pain) over and over again. A presentation which is expected to last one hour can be thought through in minutes; its style, its audience and its venue can be imagined and prepared for over and over in different ways. A look at the clock after having given these illusory talks with their multiplicity of visual aids and listeners, shows that relatively little time has passed.

The value of vivid recall is that it connects us with *memory* the facet of presentation which most alarms those of us who have to speak in public.

Try to recall, as exactly as you can, what you did last Saturday.

Note down the times when you start and finish the following exercise

Go over the day hour by hour and try not to leave anything out.

How long did it take? Some time perhaps, and though it certainly didn't take a day to recall a day, it would definitely have entailed intense concentration of a kind which we rarely use. Make vivid recall part of your habitual routine. Go to that thought-gym regularly. Use it last thing at night so that your brain can digest information while you sleep. Your memory will improve by leaps and bounds and yet another facet of the invaluable, multi headed tool which is visualisation will be safely under your belt.

LEARN BY OBSERVATION

Go to other people's presentations. Whatever the subject matter, any other presenter is worth observing. They may be acting in a play, or doing a stand-up comedy routine, they may be giving a talk or a poetry reading, or ranting at Speakers' Corner. Any situation in which one human being is trying to get a spoken message across to others is going to be of value to you. Take note of what they do, and take notes. Whatever you thought was bad, remember it, and reject it. Whatever you thought was good, and might work for you, try it out, but not as a mimic. An audience that wants to be informed doesn't need dozens of clones of Nelson Mandela, or thirty Ophra Winfreys or multiple copies of any other celebrity. Audiences are after the 'you' who has absorbed facets of other presenters' work but made them your own. People respect an original.

SEE YOURSELF AS OTHERS SEE YOU

When first we see ourselves on video, we are mesmerised either by the horror of how we look or the charm of our own presence. Whichever is the case, we are fascinated; so much so, that if other people are watching with us we immediately decry ourselves for fear that they will catch on to the fact that the only thing of interest to us is ourselves. We are capable of extending interest to another person only if they are family members or intimates. This overwhelming self interest inevitably stops us from taking in the whole picture.

You will have to watch yourself over and over again so that you can eliminate selfishness and self denigration from the frame and finally begin to see yourself as others see you. Once you have reached that stage, you will be ready to use the video as the fabulous learning aid that it is rather than as a stick with which to beat your self.

WATCH YOURSELF CLOSELY

Notice first the movements your body makes that you did not consciously initiate. There will be a lot of them.

Note them down and make choices. Which will you keep because they add to your message, and which will you definitely eliminate?

There will be some you are unsure about when first you see them, but when next you video your presentation, those 'don't knows' are likely to become clearly appropriate or clearly inappropriate for you to use.

Do the expressions that flit across your face connect with the message you are trying to convey?

Do you come across as sincere in what you say?

Do your eyes make contact with your listeners or are they glancing off to right or left trying to call the next section of your presentation to mind?

Do you lean your head to right or left as if listening intently to yourself?

Do you bat your eyelids or have any unnecessary facial twitches?

Do your hand movements distract attention from your message?

Do your hands ever obliterate part of your face?

You will find that the above activities become less noticeable if you give *all your attention* to the *meaning* of what you are saying. Video yourself again with that idea uppermost in your mind and, only after you have done that, consciously set about changing things which you still don't like. Then, video yourself again to check that the new attitudes that you have chosen are as appropriate as you intended them to be.

WATCH YOUR BACK

Most presenters are unaware of how often they turn their backs on an audience. On video the back rears up and confronts us with our discourtesy.

Do you turn your back on your audience as you go up to the white board or the black board or the flip chart and poke you face intently into the words you write there whilst ignoring the people you are supposed to be persuading to your point of view?

Do you turn away from your audience to watch the slides you are showing when you already know very well what is on those slides?

Do you seem more often to be part of your audience rather than the focus of its attention?

If you do any of those things, plan to change your way of working.

On occasion, intentionally to turn your back on an audience can be an effective presentational ploy, but only if it gets your message to the front of people's minds.

LEARN WHILE WATCHING TV

We see examples of good presentational styles on our television screens every day, and one would think that because we are so often exposed to those examples, it would be easy for us to present well at first go.

Mostly, though, we see head-and-shoulder shots of presenters. Even when we see the whole of the person, they are often sitting, or walking merely to be greeted, and then sitting. Those we see in action shots walking towards camera crews often seem ill at ease or unnaturally lively as they speak on the move.

Watch TV in order to observe how different people present themselves and their different messages and you will begin to notice things about posture, facial habits, and hands and feet, that had not struck you before. You will be able to assess whether other people's bodies add to or detract from the points they are trying to make. You will be able to make choices about how you would do their jobs if given the chance.

BECOME CONSTRUCTIVELY SELF-ABSORBED
Look at yourself from as many angles as possible, in as many places as possible. When you are out in the street, observe your reflection in shop windows and doorways.

Watch others of your own sex whose height and weight is the same as your own. Observe others of the opposite sex or from other cultures whose height and weight is the same as your own.

How do they hold themselves? How do they go up steps? How do they sit? How do they deal with other people? How do they speak? What do they sound like?

When you are no longer in the same vicinity as the person you observed, try out his or her stance, walk, expressions, voice and interactions.

Go through the barrier of feeling foolish, and keep going through it until you stop feeling foolish. Only then will you begin to learn from the experiences you are putting your body, mind and voice through.

When you have tried out a good number of other people's bodily and vocal postures start to make choices about your own body and your own voice.

Are you satisfied with how you stand and move and sound?

Does what you do with your body and your voice make for a confident stance and a pleasing tone of voice?

Does your voice respond to your mood and add to your message?

The answer to these questions should be, "yes." If it is not, use your observations of others whose actions and speech you admire, to help you to make the changes which will satisfy you.

ASK FOR FEEDBACK

Ask friends to tell you what they think of your new presentational style. Ask a few foes too! Ask someone to criticise you as you deliver an actual presentation, but get them to make notes. Even the most observant person will forget points they wanted to make about earlier parts of your presentation by the time you you've reached the end. Ask members of your audience to fill in feed back sheets. Make their job simple. Ask them to tell you what they thought was the worst point about your presentational style and what they thought was the best. Ask them to tell you what they thought was worst about your presentation's content and what they thought was best.

Despite the discomfort such feedback may entail, don't allow a natural resentment of criticism to stop you taking notice of what your critics have to say. Even those who may be trying to unnerve you can still have noticed something which will add to your performance and your message. Be grateful for comment no matter what its motive. It will help you to serve audiences better in the future.

CONSIDER YOUR MATERIAL

The sole reason for the existence of any presenter is to help an audience to get hold of ideas. Whether you are giving lectures, teaching classes, running seminars, delivering conference papers, guiding tour groups or facilitating training sessions either in real time or via video link, your major concern should be to ensure that your subject goes down well with your audience.

Writing does not constitute speech. Even a script for actors does not indicate how a part should be spoken, but only how it should be understood. When you are preparing a presentation you are your own script writer. You can set down your words in the way you would like to speak them. You can make sure that the method you devise is suited to your style of speaking and to the length of phrases you can sustain.

CREATE A SPEECH

Realise that punctuation marks are marks which make sense of written words. They do not necessarily indicate the best breathing places for spoken words.

Make sure that you mark places at which you are going to breathe. Don't ignore them. Create a script which speaks to you from the page, so that you can speak to your audience as though there was no script there at all.

Use double spacing.

Use larger sized fonts than for your usual written work.

Use UPPER CASE, *italic face*, **bold face**.

Use coloured markers to point up ideas you want to stress, or words you want to dwell on.

Use   un us u al   spa cing between sy lla bles, l e t t e r s,   words and lines   to   make your language more   LiVeLy, more *solemn* or more **emphatic!**

PAUSE FOR THOUGHT

Make sure that you plan plenty of sensible stopping points during your time in front of an audience. Pauses are necessary for you to be able to keep control of your message. They are also an essential aid to audience comprehension. *Pausesare vitaltosensepausesarevitaltosensepausesarevitaltosensepausesarevitaltosensepause sarevitaltosensepausesarevitaltosensepausesarevitaltosense:* as you can see.

There is a risk during a pause that someone may break the silence with an interjection. But if you place stopping points at sensible moments and lead up to them by raising the pitch of your voice a little so that they are an anticipated part of the phrases you are speaking, interruptions will only occur if there is someone in your audience either hell bent on disruption (and sometimes there is) or with a really valid point to make.

SPEAK OUT FROM THE WORD "GO."

As you consider text you intend to deliver to an audience, don't read it to yourself, but speak it out aloud from the moment you first see it. This will force you to notice right from the start whether listeners will be able to take in at one hearing what you have decided to tell them. You will discover straight away the points which need the greatest emphasis; the places at which you should slow down or repeat or re-phrase in order to clarify meaning. You will also immediately pinpoint places where you should alter volume or change the weight or pitch of your voice.

Speaking out from the word "go" takes a bit of getting used to. Give your self the chance to do so, however, and you will find it a most useful device.

ATTEND TO CONCENTRATION

How long should you expect another person to attend to you before that person's attention starts to slip? One way to tell is to work out how long you are able to concentrate on a topic before your own attention begins to wander.

Listen with care to a programme of spoken material.

Note down the time as you begin.

(As this is purely a listening exercise, don't use TV.)

Concentrate! Be really strict with yourself.

The moment you realise that you have lost the thread of what is being said, note down the time again.

You will probably find that despite having given the subject dedicated concentration, your attention span was not as long as you anticipated it would be.

It is salutary to realise that even the most intent audience member rarely listens with as much care as you did whilst trying out that exercise. Let that realisation help you to devise your material accordingly.

Use visual aids strategically, not merely as a running visual commentary. Insert lively verbal images. Add relevant humour. Ask relevant questions.

Place these ideas at moments when you think that your own attention span might run out, and you will be likely to maintain the interest of many more people in your audience than if you were simply to – as one author puts it – 'stand up, throw your chest out and get on with it.'

PREPARE WELL

Individual presentations always require individual preparation. However au fait you become with speaking in public, however well you know your subject, each audience has the right to expect that you will have focused in advance on its specific needs. Once you are experienced and are to talk on a subject which you know well, you may have only to focus for a few moments, but any one who talks often to groups knows that the moments dedicated to a presentation beforehand add greatly to the quality of the minutes of that presentation when it is in hand.

Yes. We all know and admire presenters who plan a whole presentation just an hour or so before they are due to speak. They may even speak off-the-cuff. But all of them will have spent many hours learning their subject and practising their presentation skills well in the first place. What is more, very few of them will not have experienced difficulty and fear when addressing an audience at some time in their careers.

As you become more practised at giving presentations you will also be able to shorten preparation time. But nothing can take away from the fact that you must know your stuff to give good presentations, and the only way to do that is to prepare, prepare, prepare and then prepare some more. Every time you have to deal with a new topic, you will have to find out about its background and work at it until you feel it belongs to you. Tedious though that may sound, you will find that the more you learn about a subject the more you become at ease with it. Tedium often turns into fascination.

PRACTISE IN ORDER TO MAKE AND MAINTAIN PERFECT

Practising will feel less tedious and be more fruitful when material you work with relates to your eventual presentation. If you are to speak about advertising a company product, then articles in the design and technology section of a newspaper are more likely to prove valuable to you than are those in the Agony

Aunt column. If your intended paper is on chaotic systems, an article on the love interest of pop stars is not going to be as helpful for you to practise on as one, say, on the latest advances in weather forecasting – though, on second thoughts, may be it is.

At least one hour's preparation for every five minutes of presentation is the recommendation from the MD of a well-known airline company to its management trainees. This is not just bloody-mindedness designed to make an already overworked employee despair of ever getting on top of the job, and it does not refer to rehearsing lines. It refers to rehearsing the body of your knowledge so that you can pull out just the right amount with which you will face an audience.

Most of us have to discipline ourselves to practise well. We discover all sorts of ways to prevaricate. But to be able to vary your menu at a moment's notice means that you must know your stuff; you must own your knowledge. Be in no doubt, if you are not well enough prepared, the person who is going to suffer most is you.

The managing director of a large Australian agri-chemical company gets his sales team to present to each other before going out to present to a client base. There is resistance to this practice from those who are new to it; they see it as a waste of time. But when they get out into the real world, they discover that – because they were well prepared – the baptism of fire which they were anticipating turns into an energising adventure.

UNAVOIDABLE TOPICS

Presenters often have to speak about subjects which are dictated by others. Do not assume that you can deliver such a presentation simply by copying what someone else did on a previous occasion and hoping for the best. The presentational style and language of one speaker rarely looks or sounds good on another, and your uncertainty about the validity of your information will inevitably dampen your energy and deflect from your message. It will also weaken your voice and make you seem inept.

If you are expected to communicate company policy with which you have little sympathy, always value yourself enough to choose your own examples and find your own ways to affect the quality of the message.

Personal study will often allow you to discover a way to deal with antipathy to a topic about which you have been instructed to speak, and enable you to give a convincing presentation. If that doesn't work for you, try to use the sensations you experienced whilst delivering a message which you did believe in, to trigger ways of putting across the one with which you have so little sympathy.

If you find that you cannot relate to your message and yet must deliver it – check by recording yourself that your tone of voice does not betray your true feelings then present your words with vigour. Deal with any questions which arise in the same manner. Be practical and business like. Make it clear. Make it short. Make it simple, and leave it at that.

CHOOSE RELEVANT MATERIAL

There are times when matters of import have to be put over or got across to an audience. Those two composite verbs tell you all you need to know about the way you, as a speaker, should deal with such material. It is true that those whose everyday work is involved with intricate subject matter and minutely detailed concepts will be used to taking in and absorbing more detail than most. But information which is too densely packaged will fog the finest mind and deaden the liveliest imagination: the very part of each person's mind that you should be aiming to trigger.

Keep in mind that a good presentation is not a showcase for everything you know, but a careful selection of items relevant to the subject and to the audience at hand. Don't pitch your subject at your audience, but pitch-in with them to uncover its fascination.

No matter what the situation, no matter how learned the group you have in front of you, aim to create a tension which will catch attention. Be seen to be juggling ideas in front of your audience. Choose your words well. Use ones that are vibrant. Avoid drab language. It can all too easily make your voice sound flat and expressionless and turn even the most interesting subject into a boring one.

MAKE THE STYLE FIT

The audience you are to address should dictate the style of your performance. If you put across news of a ground-breaking method of archaeological exploration to fellow experts in the same way as to a group attending a night school class on the rudiments of archaeology, you will certainly make one of those groups unhappy. You would, at the very least, need to change your choice of words for each group. This does not mean that you have to talk-down to one group and flatter the other. It means that you have to prepare two separate talks, utilising the same material but making sure that the language you choose lays out your subject in terms of the level of expertise your audience has attained.

Make sure that the style of your presentation fits the material being presented. A mismatch can be so off-putting that it can render your words meaningless. Imagine Bjork or Robbie Williams singing Nineteenth Century Opera in their own vocal idioms, or Callas or Pavarotti performing the blues bel canto, and you will get some idea of how disconcerting such a presentation can be. Perhaps that's what happened in the Tower of Babel. Maybe each person was speaking the same language but trying to put across ideas in such an inappropriate manner that the words came out as senseless babble.

PUT JARGON IN ITS PLACE

As a presenter, you will often be speaking about a specific subject and your topic will use terminology known to others who work in the same field. Such audiences will expect you to use the language of the discipline, but even for initiates, the use of too much jargon can be a turn-off. Should you be aware that your audience contains novices in the field or strangers to your site take particular care to define your terms or devise a handout with clear definitions to which the uninitiated can refer as you speak. If you are naming concepts new to an audience, give your listeners time to absorb them. Names contain the very nature of things and should be allowed to register in a listener's mind.

ADD VARIETY

To help your message to be accessible to as many people as possible, it should be made up from a variety of materials. It should contain loose knit and densely woven sections of variegated textures and patterns.

If each layer merely discloses another of the same weave your presentation will lose the titillating, tantalising qualities which should pervade even the most obtuse subject matter, the most banal topic.

One device which will assist you to add variety is to add colour. This does not mean that you should be 'seeing red' as you give your presentations or 'feeling blue,' but rather that you should persuade people to value the points you make by colouring the tone of voice you use to make them.

Play with the following adverbs:

warmly, scathingly, interestingly, confidentially, boringly, passionately, angrily.

Apply these to your manner of speaking as you practise various texts.

Such topics as *'The Peat Bogs of Western Europe'* delivered warmly and passionately can stir an audience no end!

ADD A TOUCH OF HUMOUR

Humour is an important aid to understanding and can add welcome levity to weighty material. But a presentation is neither the time nor the place to develop a stand-up comedy routine; too many laughs leave an audience bemused. Jokes without relevance to the topic in hand should be avoided. An audience's laughter at them may stroke your vanity, but the fact is that such laughter puts you at a disadvantage as a presenter, because it deliberately deflects the audience from thinking about the substance of your presentation.

BREAK DOWN AUDIENCE RESISTENCE

A good presentation should make the hearts within an audience beat with lively interest, not chug along with boring predictability. Indeed, there is scientific evidence that the heightening of emotions breaks down a body's resistance to the acceptance of change. Propagandists have been putting this knowledge to use for centuries. Put it to use yourself. It will invigorate you, and increase the ability of your audiences to get hold of your ideas which is, after all, the sole reason for the existence of any presentation.

BE YOUR OWN STAGE MANAGER

It stands to reason that no matter who you are or what form of presentation you have to give, if you don't find out in advance about the space you are to speak in and whether your hosts possess the equipment you are planning to use, you will have a bad experience. If you turn up at an unknown venue half an hour before you are due to speak, you will have to hare about getting your act together. And you may not make it in time; so, take a leaf out of a jobbing actor's book.

Forget all that you have heard about personal agents who arrange venues, advertising, ticketing and accommodation; or production managers who oversee all scenic and lighting matters; or stage managers who drive the artist to the venue, move furniture, lay out props, organise costumes, sweep the set, and keep members of the public at bay until the performance begins. The fact is that jobbing actors organise all of that stuff themselves. What is more they arrive at the venue early enough to ensure that once they have set things in place they can then try out the acoustic and rehearse. They then leave the space well before the audience arrives and reappear to give a performance which shows no sign of any problem which may have occurred during the get-in process.

To help you to give just such a problem free performance follow the advice in the paragraph below and then pick and choose from the indented paragraphs after it. You should find something amongst the thirty ideas which will help you to stage manage the types of presentation you have to deliver.

ARRANGE THINGS IN ADVANCE

Liaise with each venue about all practical matters. On the basis of the information you receive take all necessary equipment with you. Once at the venue, with or without help from a resident technician, transfer everything you need into the space you are to work in. Make sure that seating for your anticipated audience is where you want it; if necessary, arrange it yourself. Check that all your equipment works and rehearse, or top and tail, what you are to say in the space in which you are to host your audience. If possible vacate the space before your listeners start to come in so that you have time to collect your thoughts.

A STAGE MANAGEMENT CHECK LIST

■ Spend time and energy finding out how to get to your venue and make sure that there is a contact telephone number and someone at the end of it who knows about your projected visit. If you want to use a photocopier make sure that one will be available and free when you need it.

■ View the space in which you are going to work in advance if you can. If that's not possible, ask for a plan of the space and its contents early enough for you to arrange to have furniture, screens etc. arranged to your satisfaction.

■ If you are expected to speak from a raised platform, find out how high it is, how many steps lead up to it, and what its proportions are. Is there going to be room for you to move about? Are there objects on the platform that cannot be moved? Practise within those confines.

■ Check what is behind you in the space. A window through which other activities can be seen to be taking place may distract your audience and be a cause of unnecessary embarrassment to you.

■ Never work with light or sun behind you. It is most distracting for an audience and tiring for their eyes. Turn everything round if necessary

■ Make sure that tea breaks and so on are arranged to fit with your plans. Otherwise, trolleys, cups and saucers can appear at very inappropriate moments and cause prolonged distraction.

■ Check well in advance that equipment which you are planning to use for your slides and overheads is available at the venue and compatible with your stuff.

■ Have your own slide carousel(s) and cartridges. Place any slides you are to use in their correct order before you leave home and run them through quickly at the venue well before your audience arrive.

■ Keep the slides and all your overheads and your lap top in your own possession until you get up to speak. Nothing will throw you more than finding that visual aids are in the wrong order or have gone missing.

■ Carry screwdrivers, appropriate electrical spares and a spare extension lead with you.

■ Take your own sets of pens for writing on acetates and white boards – and remember which is which. Take old fashioned chalk too! Choose pens with blue, black or dark green ink. The colour red is difficult for audiences to see.

■ As soon as you arrive at your destination, try out your voice in the space you are to work in. Where you find dry resonance, plan to pitch your voice a little higher than usual. In a reverberant space plan to emphasise consonants strongly and to speak more slowly than you would normally do.

■ If at all possible, make it your responsibility to ensure that your space is well ventilated.

■ Know where light switches and plugs are and which lights and equipment they operate. Keep light levels as high as possible. You need to be able to see your audience, to gauge its reaction, and though you want your audience to see your slides it also needs to see you. What is more, human beings tend to fall asleep when it is dark.

■ Take note of the old Chinese proverb: "People with little knowledge use many slides." Let's say, as a rule of thumb, no more than ten to twelve slides per 40 minutes of presentation.

■ Carry a small clock with a clear face with you to keep an eye on timing. If you are going to use your watch, take it off and put it where you can see its face. There is nothing more distracting to an audience than seeing a presenter checking his or her wrist whilst speaking.

■ When you are writing on flip charts during a presentation, hug the easel around its back with your left hand and write across your body with your right hand. Left handers: stand on the opposite side and hug with your right hand. From this position, you will be able to keep an eye on your audience and see when it becomes necessary to reiterate or rephrase what you are saying.

■ Black boards and white boards tend to be fixed to walls. When you are writing on them, keep your left hip against the board and step forward with your left foot first. Walk along the board in this way, writing across your body as you go. Again this enables you to watch out for your audience and make sure that they can follow your line of thought. It helps with discipline too.

Left handed people have a bit of a problem with this technique because it entails having to walk right hip against the board and backwards. On a raised platform, make sure that you work out how many paces you can safely take before you fall off the other end.

■ Whether you are left or right handed always have some way of cleaning a board before you begin. Carry your own bottle of water or cleaning fluid and a cloth if necessary. It is arrogant to assume that an audience is going to be prepared to follow your line of thought, however erudite, through a maze of irrelevant material from previous sessions.

Students in the computer department of at least one famous university regularly have to put up with such discourtesy.

■ If you decide to write onto acetates during a presentation have a plentiful supply with you so that you do not feel constrained to cover any one of them too densely. WRITE LARGE. Make only points which will clarify or amplify what you are saying.

■ Prepare in advance acetates containing the concepts, dates, algorithms or mathematical equations which constitute your main argument.

■ Beware that the fun of working with 'Power Point' doesn't beguile you into producing too many slides filled with excessive bullet points which simply befuddle an audience.

■ The delight of having a laser pointer in your hand should not lure you into focusing on unnecessary information.

■ If you are to use a lap top, take care that you don't join the ranks of the techno-bores. Some presenters become so mesmerised by the box of tricks which they have programmed to perform for them that they ignore their audiences completely.

■ If you are to work from notes, make sure that they are either bound in a hard-backed folder, or printed on firm card which you have treasury tagged together. Nervous-hand-quivers as you turn your pages then won't be noticeable to your listeners and neither you nor they will be distracted by the sight of notes floating to the floor.

■ Lecterns are designed to support a script not to prop up a speaker.

■ If you are going to present to colleagues around a table, more often than not you'll find yourself hemmed in. If there is no space to use a flip chart or over-heads or to set up a screen for slides, prepare cards which you can prop it up in front of you and angle towards different members of the group. Make sure these are at least A3 size and that each card is not too densely packed with information.

Alternatively, prepare numbered handouts and ask people to go through them with you in a sequence which you will indicate. If you choose this method, expect the silence which reading will necessitate. Expect a bit of chat too, but don't allow that to deflect the group from the rest of your message. There will always be some people who will ignore instructions and leaf through hand-outs following their own agenda. If you feel that this would throw you, don't set yourself up for it to happen.

■ If you are to use a fixed microphone you need someone to suggest where you should stand or sit for optimum sound quality. Once a fixed mike's parameters have been set, you will have to remember not to sway around during your presentation or your words will sway out of earshot.

■ If possible seat yourself in the auditorium and get someone else to speak through the mike, then you can get some idea of whether the sound level set is the one you want.

■ If you place your mouth too close to fixed or hand microphones the consonants "p" and "b" will plop, and the consonants "s" – "t" – "d" – "f" – "k" can become explosions which blot out your message entirely.

■ When you use a hand held microphone avoid clutching it in a vice like grip as the tension in your grasp will communicate itself to the whole of your body.

Think of it, rather, as an ice cream cone. Hold it firmly but level with the front of your chin, the dome of the cone just below, but not touching, your bottom lip.

Keep it in that position and all your words will be clearly heard while any strong consonants, sharp intakes of breath, coughs or throat-clearing will flow over its head.

■ Watch out! Lapel microphones attached to wires can all too easily tie you up in knots.

PERFORM YOUR PRESENTATION

The mere fact of standing in front of a group which waits to hear you confers powerful properties upon you. It compels people's attention. It draws their gaze. It robes you in status. The moment you draw breath to speak, your audience, collectively, holds its breath. Such power is without price, yet it is conferred upon any person who has the privilege to address a group of others who are waiting to hear what is to be said. To choose to ignore that moment of power is wilfully to refuse to unlock the door to a treasure house though you hold the key in your own hand.

You may find yourself in a vast, raked auditorium with a sea of faces rising above you where you have to take a long walk even before you get to the point from which you are going to begin your presentation. You may be in a cramped room filled with a central table and chairs past which you have to squeeze and then present your information to the whites of your colleagues' eyes. In either case, your audience will begin to assess you from the moment they see you.

MAKE AN ENTRANCE

It is not for nothing that actors practise entrances. They know that how you appear as you appear affects the whole of a performance. They know that to gain the attention of any audience its members must immediately be made aware that they are in the company of competent players.

Make use of that knowledge for yourself. Take the floor as soon as you appear. Fill the space as soon as you begin to speak. Realising that it is in safe hands, your audience will instantly relax and attend to your message.

CONTROL YOUR NERVES

Performance, then, is submission to the scrutiny and judgement of others. To do that takes courage. If for you, as for many presenters, the thought of being in front of an audience throws you into a panic, there is a way to calm your fear.

Imagine that you are a member of your own audience.

Visualise yourself out there, bang in the middle of the group.

Speak to yourself as you sit out there.

Engage with yourself and you will engage with other members of you audience. But do not, even for one moment, allow yourself to think that the topic on which you are about to speak will be boring. That tinge of uncertainty will communicate itself instantly to your expectant listeners.

VOICE YOUR THOUGHTS

When first you open your mouth to speak, you will disadvantage yourself greatly if people have to listen while you clear your throat. Whatever you have been doing before you face an audience you must make sure that your voice skims out cleanly.

Just before you get up to speak and before you get on mike – if you are using one – say one low, *"Hmmmmmm,"* and one high, *"Hmmmmmm,"* quite strongly to yourself.

The flexing of your vocal cords which creates the pitch change should shift any frog lurking in your throat, and you will have the comfort of knowing that your voice exists.

Breathe Out. Allow air to flow in. Begin your presentation.

Begin your presentation with a sentence which is pithy and relevant to your topic then dive in to your subject with an elegant far reaching dive so that people can perceive your trajectory, don't immediately disappear down into the depths before they have had a chance to take stock of you.

Believe that what makes sense in your head will make sense in your mouth and make an impact on your audience. Vary the tune of your words to help listeners to get your message more easily. Intend to be heard and you will be heard.

CONSIDER YOUR AUDIENCE

Approach your audience benignly. Gain their sympathy. Smile at them with your eyes. Take in the space you are about to fill with your words.

Visualise a comfortably distant horizon that curves
behind the furthest members of your audience.

**Look out to that horizon from time to time during your presentation.
Speak to its curvilinear distance.**

Even when you are addressing colleagues with whom you are extremely familiar, don't allow yourself to be distracted from the idea that you are giving a performance.

You may feel that a bit of banter in the board room or conviviality in the Common-room will relax everyone. But, though you are part of a team under normal circumstances, your position on this occasion marks you out and thrusts you into heroic mode. Take your position seriously. Even if the group contains people who are much higher up the hierarchical ladder than you, during your presentation, you are in charge. Courteously deflect stuff which is not relevant. Courteously deflect stuff which is deliberately subversive. Bullying usually stops if it encounters strength.

CONSIDER YOUR PERFORMANCE

A good actor in a good solo performance draws listeners in to a story, fills them in on its plot, brings everything to a conclusion and – even if there is a twist in the tale – does not lose contact with the audience until the show is over. A good presenter in a good presentation should do exactly the same.

But a presenter cannot become a different character. Whatever the circumstance which led to your having to stand up in public, it is *you,* performing as a larger than life *you,* who must find ways to educate and enrich, interest, and entice your audience and give life to your presentation, no matter how complex its subject – matter may be. You can, however, try out different personality traits from the ones you care to show in everyday life as you practise, and these may well help you to loosen up and be more comfortable with the craft of performance. You can also learn from the example set by those who have turned the craft into an art.

The Nobel Prize winning physicist, Richard Feynman, was able to put across extremely difficult concepts to his students. They understood him even though they knew that they did not have the intellectual tools to explain such ideas for them-selves. He allowed his audiences to peep through keyholes from which they could glimpse realms beyond their present scope. He placed key concepts within their grasp and enticed them to try to unlock the doors of understanding for themselves.

He did what great teachers have done from time immemorial. He used known quantities to quantify the unknown. He used descriptions of common things to explain the exotic.

Interestingly – from the point of view of the emphasis of this book – he chose the idea of his own voice speaking, to illustrate how a photon comes into being.

'When an atom makes a transition from one state to another it emits a particle of light called a photon. "It's like the sound that I'm making now. It wasn't in me before."'

To describe himself, Feynman made use of poetry.

> atoms with consciousness;
> matter with curiosity.
>
> stands at the sea,
> wonders at wondering: I
> a universe of atoms
> an atom in the universe.

[What Do <u>You</u> Care What Other People Think? Richard P. Feynman: Unwin, 1988.]

Observe from that poem, something common to all great communicators. They are not afraid to use sentimentality. They move easily from humour to pathos. They have an ability to speak of things in a way designed to get a listener's emotions quickly stirred; the tear ducts to flow; the hairs to tingle at the nape of the neck; the chill of correction to be plainly felt. They stir themselves to emotion, and are not ashamed to show it. Aim to take on an emotional persona when you present, and make it your own.

LEARN TO EMOTE

How on earth does one practise to emote? It is such a difficult thing to do that the very mention of it makes most people, especially those from Western cultures, feel highly embarrassed. If only there was some way of easing the extreme self-consciousness of undertaking the task.

Ideally, use a video recorder to capture your movements as you do this exercise.

Take a sheet of A4 or Letter paper and squeeze the two sides of it together at the bottom edges to create a handle.

You will find that the rest of the page has formed itself into a curve, and that you have a speedily improvised mask.

Speak about any topic from behind that page.

Take yourself seriously and speak using strong emotions: terror, fury, disgust, guile, dejection, delight, amusement, hysteria, thrill, boredom, hatred.

Those strong emotions will seem pretty strange if you were using them to speak about the *History of Management Structures within the Live Stock Industry,* or *Good Practice in Supermarket Shelving,* but they will be training your voice and body into a lively awareness of a variety of muscular processes without you realising how rigorous such training is.

Play back the video and observe what you were doing during that vocal tour de force. Were you convincing or do you need to delve deeper into the character of each emotion?

Now, summon up the courage to watch as you do the exercise again without the mask in front of your face.

Your expressions in your mirror or on your video will probably both horrify you and make you fall about laughing because you are so close to them. But if you are to give a presentation to a lot of people in a large space, a certain amount of facial exaggeration is necessary to your performance and to your voice; and by putting your facial muscles through this baptism of fire they will at least be getting accustomed to being used in an expansive way.

BE EFFICIENT

Giving a presentation is a tiring activity. Speaking and standing for long periods are both unusual muscular activities. No serious actor would take on a sustained role without some fitness training and neither should a serious presenter. It takes practice to stand speaking for long periods so don't be surprised if your throat, back and legs ache by the time you have finished.

Know that to stand upright, head supported by the shoulders, feet apart, one foot slightly in front of the other, knees slack will keep you balanced however long you have to be on your feet.

Learn not to equate the energy you expend with how well your performance is going down with your audience. Many presenters when trying to get a point across feel that they must be seen to be writing away and busy. They behave as if they are in a farce and by the end of a session are worn out from their active participation with flip charts, slides, pens, laser pointers or chalk. It is true that writing something down rather than merely reading it assists learning but a presenter should gain that benefit during the unseen writing of preparation not while persuading an audience to follow a particular way of thinking.

BAN PATHETIC CONCLUSIONS

Too many excellent presentations unravel in their last moments. The pattern of argument, so carefully laid out, just frays away because so little attention is paid to securing the final knot. Sometimes the message has been cast aside, the body has sagged, the head has lowered, the voice has faded away, and a presenter has sat down, before even the most attentive listener has realised that the presentation is over. The attentive listener has been cheated and has every right to feel dissatisfied. The presenter has fallen down on the job. The performance has not been concluded. It has been halted in its tracks. What a let down! Don't do that to your audience. Don't do that to yourself.

Plan from the beginning how you are going to end your presentation. Make sure that the final section is proportionate to the whole and truly conclusive. Flag-up the fact that you are only going to continue for a brief while longer, then summarise the main points of your argument. Who knows, relief that the presentation is almost finished may even catch inattentive listeners off guard and cause them unwittingly to take in the gist of what you have been saying. You do not have to end on a 'high;' you can end on a 'low,' but that low should reveal depths still to be plumbed.

Even as you sit down or step away from your audience or give way to another speaker remain in performance mode. Allow your conclusion and your voice to resonate well after you have spoken your final word.

ADJUST TO THE DEMANDS OF THE OCCASION

Audience members, without exception, will be in different states of preparedness for what you are going to say. Each person will have a particular way of listening-to and taking-in what they hear. Each will have encountered teaching in some form during their lives, and the nature of those encounters will either hamper or assist the way that they respond to you. For these and other reasons, your own feelings of satisfaction or dissatisfaction with your performance often bear no relationship to what has gone on in the minds of those listening to you.

Every audience will contain people who are not happy to be where they are. There will be those who may be ill or preoccupied with self-worries or jet lagged or drunk or drugged or just plain sleepy. There will be those bored with *any* topic, scathing of *any* presenter and filled to deafness with their own knowledge; yet others may be plagued with actual deafness.

Keep in mind as we consider ways in which to deliver the different types of presentation on the following pages, that though your job is to alleviate all of the above conditions and to encourage even the most wilfully inattentive person to gain from your message, what your listeners then do with what you have said is not your responsibility.

GIVING LECTURES

Lectures inevitably take longer when you get up and speak them for real, than they do when you practise them in the car, at the office, or in the bathroom at home, so for an hour's lecture about 50 minutes of speaking time in practice conditions is likely to be sufficient.

Overheads, slides, white boards, flip charts are not there as aides-mémoires for you – though that may be a bonus of their existence. Visual aids were designed to benefit members of an audience. Unless you are lecturing to non English speakers, people do not need the whole text of what you are saying in front of them. Just a few key points.

Lectures often take place in a tiered space, which means that you have to look up to see the people at the back. You may be tempted not to look to the back at all; but that is not an option. You may be tempted to raise your chin and stretch your neck to focus upwards. Avoid that posture. It will tire your voice too easily. Think of the back row as the brow of a hill. Step back from the group as far as you are able and slacken your knees a little. Speak as if to a crowd of listeners sitting over the brow of the hill on the same level as your eye line. Your words will then carry on an all embracing arc of sound.

Set a problem or pose a question relevant to your topic and ask your audience members to consider how they would unravel that problem or answer that question.

Direct them to speak with the person to their left or to their right, or in front of them or behind them. Don't forget to allow for odd numbers and row ends. Even in raked lecture theatres, and with very large audiences it is possible to work in this way

Allot a couple of minutes or so for the members of your audience to share thoughts and opinions.

These tactics are useful because they empower an audience and make its members feel that they have something to do in a situation where they may have expected merely to be passive.

Unless you have devised a way to make the answers which your audience comes up with a meaningful part of your presentation, you don't need to know what they said. Just let people talk to refresh themselves. Speaking ensures that people take in more breath than if they were silent. The increased oxygen gives them energy and helps them, quite naturally, to be more ready to listen to what you have to say. Such an exchange will be especially useful if your presentation comes straight after lunch or at the end of a group of sessions. It helps with both digestion and fatigue.

Be prepared for the amount of noise that a group of people speaking together will create. It can be alarmingly loud.

To regain the attention of a large group, pre-arrange that you will, say, flick a light switch as a signal that you wish to move on.

With smaller groups, interrupt people by coming in strongly, and at a different pitch than that of the general hubbub.

Use phrases such as: *"Right then,* shall we move on?"

"Well now, *let's think about our next move?"*

"O.K. *let's get going."*

The two introductory words delivered strongly will clear people's ears to take-in the instruction contained in the second part of each sentence. This will prepare them to listen further. Don't wait for absolute silence but as the hubbub subsides indicate some of the answers which you might have given to the question you posed or the puzzle you set. Then, when people are really attentive, give some clues about the direction you intend to take and whether you are going to give time for questions at the end, and then set off on your lecture.

Some speakers, especially when in raked lecture theatres, talk only to people easily in sight. They may even fix on just one member of the audience. This causes considerable embarrassment to the person who has become the arbitrary object of the lecturer's attention, and cuts off anyone outside the speaker's immediate compass. Every listener should get the feeling as they listen to you that they are involved in a two way process. Inexperienced members of your audience, apprentices, students, extreme novices should feel excited by the glimpses of the knowledge which you now share with them and which they hope to own in greater detail as they gain experience. Members of your audience who already outstrip you in the area of your expertise should be able to see from the trajectory of your argument how it could project their own work further.

Think long and hard about how you are going to conclude your lecture. Allow no less than one eighth of your allotted time and make sure that the conclusion contains a summary of the main points you have made.

Don't just slink away, but wrap up proceedings cleanly. Your audience members then know that they can ask questions or leave without appearing rude.

DELIVERING CONFERENCE PAPERS

Simply to read out a paper which has been prepared for publication is to court disaster. Do not let the fact that some older or more learned people deliver papers in this way convince you that it is the right thing to do. Venerate those people for their knowledge and experience, not for their poor presentation skills.

Work which is written to be read is always too dense to be spoken and is a complete turn-off for an audience. A paper due for publication is far too detailed to be read out in its entirety to an audience. Yes. You may be the author of that paper, but during its presentation, you are the speaker whose ideas are being heard, not the writer whose ideas are being read.

However interested in, and conversant with your subject an audience may be, a close reading from a podium bound colleague will just bore the pants off them. Those who know that you are going to read out your paper won't even bother to come to hear you. They will wait until the work appears in print and read it for themselves.

The ideal way to present at a conference is to talk about the main ideas your paper contains. If you are too inexperienced or too scared to ad lib about your work in that way, then you should either reformat your paper as a script that suits your delivery and your style of speech, or write out a 'speakable' synopsis. Alternatively, get help from an editor or ask a more experienced colleague to devise your wording for you.

At the best conferences, participants gain equally from the formal and the informal proceedings because speakers keep to allotted presentation times and so can share and exchange more information during those times.

Unless you are to be the keynote speaker, you will usually be given no more than 15 minutes to present a paper. That means fifteen minutes at most. Be assured that a speech which takes fifteen minutes every time you rehearse it, will invariably takes half as long again when you present it in the cold light of day. Encourage yourself to be a good time keeper.

If you are to use visual aids make sure that you have practised with them in advance and know that they fit into the time slot available to you. Make sure that they add to your argument and are not merely props for your memory

Even if there is a discussant for your session, take control of your time in front of an audience. It is only common courtesy, however, to let the other person know clearly, from your manner and your words that you are nearing the end of your paper.

When you have finished speaking, let there be a beat or two of silence before you ask if anyone wishes to comment. Then, wait for a further beat or two and scan your audience in case there is someone trying to catch your attention. If there is still silence say clearly that your presentation is over, and either sit down or walk away.

DEALING WITH QUESTIONS

After questions have been called for, allow people legitimate thinking time. The peculiarly expectant silence which always ensues may worry you; if it does, fill it by working out a question in your own mind which you would ask if you were in your own audience.

Always repeat questions audibly while facing the body of your audience so that everyone can then take part in the exchange of ideas.

Deal with questioners thoughtfully and courteously. Help less able questioners by summarising what they asked you in a succinct way, but make sure that you summarise the question that was asked.

Take particular care not to insert an answer to a question which you wish someone had asked. If the matter is that important, it should have been incorporated into the body of your presentation.

Never ignore a person whose query is not pertinent to the matter in hand, or whose point is deliberately obtuse. Answer briefly and then move on.

If you do not understand what someone asks don't get flustered but get them to re-phrase their question until you do.

Have the courage to admit that you do not have the answer for some of the questions you are asked.

Even if you are answering a question which one person has asked, it is bad practice to attend solely to that person. Acknowledge the individual when first you respond, and from time to time during your answer, but always make sure that the whole of your response to any question reaches the whole of your audience.

PRESENTING VIA VIDEO LINK

Video Conferencing suddenly became much more widely used after September 11th 2001 because of the risks associated with real time travel. Many presenters must now face up to the very different risks associated with appearing on screen.

Video conference presentations are peculiarly exhausting. Unless you stay attentive during the whole of the time that the camera is running, you open yourself to ridicule. On video link audiences will either be watching you intently on a small TV screen or seeing a larger than life you projected on screen in such close-up that mere tinges of uncertainty will be seen as major insecurities. If you lose concentration, for example, your eyes go blank and everyone watching knows that that has happened.

Under normal circumstances, a good presenter looks out for the reactions of an audience. Even when the topic of a presentation requires intense concentration the presenter 'plays' the audience, assesses its reactions and aims to give its participants a good time. But on a video link there is no live audience and you get no live feed back. There's lots of energy going out, but none coming back in. Indeed, you may even be alone and working with pre-set equipment in a studio in the middle of the night because you are in a different time zone from the conference participants to whom you are speaking. To cap it all, sometimes the connection will go down without your being aware of it.

Would that it was true to tell you that you just have to behave naturally under such conditions; unfortunately, presenting via video link is a most unnatural process and requires professional help. If you can't get hold of any, you will have to gain experience by trial and error.

Set a video running and, preferably with someone else watching and scoring you as well, put yourself through as many unlikely speaking and listening scenarios as you can and give yourself marks out of ten.

Go through a number of practise runs and watch
yourself like a hawk. Observe particularly closely how you look
when you are doing listening.

Practise how to respond to funny questions – both the humorous
and the peculiar variety – so that you know what kind of expression
your face takes on at such times and can alter it if necessary.

Practise how you might react if you hadn't got the foggiest notion
of what you had been asked by a questioner, or what caused a
distant audience to fall about with laughter.

Be prepared to make a fool of yourself in front of yourself in order to avoid doing so
in front of a live audience.

RUNNING SEMINARS

A seminar is an arena for information exchange where the topic is shaped to fit
the requirements of everyone taking part.

You should aim to assist each individual within the group to realise that if everyone
is prepared to buy-in to the joint venture, his or her own knowledge will expand by
leaps and bounds rather than by tottering, solitary steps. To this end, it is best to
allot time at the outset to allow participants to decide between themselves the
format which the meeting, or meetings, should take.

To be genuinely productive seminars need an informed facilitator prepared to take
responsibility for the subject under discussion and prepared to step-in to avoid
faltering moments from becoming embarrassingly long. You will discover that
every group you work with will require different handling.

Don't be afraid of the silence which thinking before responding necessitates, but
don't allow the silence which intimidates the least knowledgeable in a group. Do

not use silence to punish those you suspect have not done preparatory work for a session since that will discomfort everyone.

When members are verbally reticent, it can be useful to do a bit of mental and vocal limbering up at the beginning of some of the early sessions.

> Divide the group into twos. Get each person to work out a tongue twister or maybe a limerick based on the topic for the session and teach it to their partner.
>
> Get each person to take it in turn to teach their partner's words to the whole group.
>
> Get them to make sure that the *sense* of the words they are passing on is uppermost in people's minds.

These exercises ensure that everyone present has to think and talk about something to do with the seminar topic, that each person has to speak up and take charge of the group, and that each person has to take responsibility for faithfully passing on another colleague's words. What is more, the stretching and flexing of the voice, face and body muscles which occurs during these activities energizes everyone from the start. There is a further advantage to be gained. People who have shared something funny together will be much more ready to share something serious. Seminars will bomb along.

GUIDING TOUR GROUPS

Make clear in your introductory remarks the estimated length of your tour and the key points you intend to include. Uppermost in your mind should be how to best to present the people in front of you with relevant and interesting information rather than digging up all the knowledge you own and dumping it on them.

Indicate, right from the start, that people should feel free to break away if they wish.

Allow those who may need to separate from your tour at some point, to feel at ease when they do so. About half way through your tour, again offer people the chance to leave if they wish. Then indicate how much longer you expect to be and, especially if you are guiding out of doors, how far the distance you have left to cover.

Lead with your mouth. Face your group when explaining where you intend to move to. Speak first. Indicate the way, and then turn to go.

Your group should never be in tow. When you move to another place you should wait until even the last stragglers have you in their sights. You should always be able to see the whites of your clients' eyes when you address them.

If you are working in congested city conditions, breathe through your nose whenever possible. Nostrils were designed to filter out dirt and equalise the temperature of air outside your body with that inside it. Taking in air in this way will protect your voice: a tour guide's most vital asset.

Whenever possible, place yourself and your group as far away from traffic as you are able. Hedges trees and walls are surprisingly effective baffles and filters. Get your groups behind such barriers if you can, or speak to them on side-streets.

If it is windy, speak with the wind behind you. This will help to carry your message to your straining listeners. If it is sunny, make sure the sun's rays are in your eyes, not in theirs.

Speak deliberately in outdoor conditions. Watch the group closely and use your lips in a more exaggerated way than you would normally do. Speak to them as though they need to lip-read. Some of them may well need to do just that.

If you must be on main roads, place your group to face the traffic whilst you stand with your back to it. Your own back will then act as a shield for your voice against fumes, and as a sounding board for your audience against traffic noise. If possible, stand with your back against a lamp post or a tree trunk or, a parked vehicle. These hard surfaces will act as extra sounding boards for you.

Even when you are not in earshot of traffic, there are sounds with which you will have to compete if you are speaking outdoors. Lawn-mowers, tractors, chain-saws, strimmers are often in evidence. There may be helicopters or aeroplanes passing overhead. Splashing fountains, waterfalls or chattering magpies may vie with you for attention. Usually, however, all such sounds are intermittent and easily avoided. But if you do have to stand your ground and compete, stand firm and pitch your voice above or below that of the interference.

Whenever it is possible stand at a slightly higher level than that of the group. This practice gives you a vantage-point and helps the group to hear you. It would be best not to stand on benches which may break under your weight, or to stand on walls which may do the same. Use steps or inclines. If you must stand lower than your group, make sure that your neck and chin are not stretched so that your Adam's apple is being pulled taut and out of alignment. Step a little further away from your group in order to achieve a better posture. Keep your knees loose. Ask the group not to crowd in on you.

Make sure that you are aware of all the movements that you make, and that all those movements add to your message. Don't sway about as you speak, or hop from foot to foot, or wave your arms like a windmill unless you have a reason to do so. Avoid bending down as you speak. Bend to indicate something – straighten up – and then speak. Avoid looking upwards as you speak. Point and look upwards – return to your former position – and then speak.

Your group will want time to absorb what you say, so avoid talking for more than 10 minutes at any one stretch and allow time for people just to look about them. Take care not to force-feed them. Whet their appetites. Give one or two meaty chunks and a good few titbits. If they want more they will ask for it.

When you use names pass them on with special respect and care. Should a number of the members of your tour group compliment you on your memory for dates and names, however, it is usually a sign that you are mentioning too many.

Care sufficiently about the information you are giving to put it across in your own way. People can always tell when a guide has learned information parrot fashion, and will always be more interested and appreciative when you give something of yourself. That does not mean that you should make up information. If you don't know something – say so. Informed speculation with a keen group can be intriguing, but make sure that the group understands that it is speculation.

When people can hear easily they attend willingly. In echoing surroundings you will have to assess the reverberation time of the space, and allow yourself to speak as slowly as that dictates. This will seem very mannered to you at first, but such carefulness will definitely pay off as far as your tour group is concerned. When indoors avoid standing on carpets. Floor-boards or tiles or any solid flooring will act as a spring-board for your voice and help to project your words to your audience.

If there are other visitors looking around who are not with your group, leave room for them to manoeuvre around you. Always wait until they have finished looking at a section or an object you wish to speak about before you begin to do so. Don't intimidate them or force them to become members of your party. On the other hand, do allow them to listen-in for a moment or two if they wish. Be prepared to change your plans and move on if necessary.

When you are describing objects stand facing your listeners not the artefact, painting or sculpture to which you refer. You should know its detail sufficiently well to have it in your mind's eye. Avoid standing where you are silhouetted in the light from a window, or where there is electric light or light from candles just behind you. It is difficult for people to see your face in such situations, and tiring for their eyes.

Smile in a warm and friendly way on frequent occasions. Make people aware that you are glad to be spending time with them. They, in turn, will discover that they genuinely enjoy your tour.

FACILITATING TRAINING SESSIONS

It is always helpful to give an outline of the overall strategy for the full training period before any sessions begin. Clients then know what they are in for. Work out that strategy so that it involves you in speaking for no more than ten minutes before introducing some change of pace, some other activity, some other medium, some other voice. Make sure that the key points you wish people to take away with them are reiterated at regular intervals – though not word for word – during your sessions.

Use visual aids to assist you but don't let any one of them take you and your session over. Check your equipment well in advance of your session. Have a fall back position. Even for computer based sessions you should carry hard copy with you in case of malfunction.

Wrap up your information in interesting parcels which you unpack before your audience. Allow them to have the fun of unpacking some of the information for themselves either as one large group or split into smaller groups.

Invent ways to add a touch of competition to these purposive games of discovery, but do not create combative situations unless they are to be of genuine value. Advertise in advance that such situations are to be a part of your training sessions.

Never knowingly reduce someone to tears. To do so is a sign of your own inadequacy.

People who attend training sessions do not need a guru or a nurse, but a competent facilitator of a learning process.

Some people who come to a training session expecting to be addressed within a group feel intimidated if you try to get them to respond individually in some way. Be aware of the 'feel' of a group. Make sure that you are always able to accommodate and encompass those who do not wish to be actively involved.

Let people know in advance if you are going to be working physically so that they can dress casually or bring clothes to change into. Give a clear idea of the appropriateness of this to the training. On the whole you will find that most people who dress formally for work on a day-to-day basis relish a more carefree approach at a training session.

Plan in advance how to accommodate anyone who chooses not to dress informally.

You are responsible for the style of your own session but you must gain permission to work closely with individuals in a group and gage when it is acceptable to do so.

Respond promptly to signals from any person who seems threatened by your presence and move away, but do so graciously, and with a warm smile so that they do not feel disadvantaged.

Your job is to assist everyone in your sessions to a better understanding of your line of business, not to a better realisation of your preferred method of working.

Keep everyone busy and involved. The best learning is always hard work but enjoyable and the last thing you want is for your clients to go away feeling that the day has been wasted.

Beware! Those who work regularly with groups know that a plan which worked wonderfully with one set of clients will sometimes come a cropper with another. A good trainer needs a butterfly mind firmly tethered to a clear understanding of the purpose of the training. Endlessly flexible, a good trainer learns how to be all things to all people, and yet still is prepared to get it wrong.

AFTER THOUGHTS

Try as you may, there is nothing you can do to avoid the prejudice of some audience members. No matter how well you have done, there may be people who just do not like the cut of your jib or the sound of your voice. That's a fact of life. There are also times when the most carefully prepared presentations by the most able presenters go less well than expected. If that happens to you, accept it as another fact of life. Everyone has a bad day from time to time. Be prepared to laugh at yourself and forgive yourself. Keep the event in your memory long enough to learn from the mistakes you made – then forget it, and live to present well another day.

OVER TO YOU

All that is left now is for you to get out there and 'do' talking. Regulate each pulse of breath so that your listeners catch your every word. Lift up your voice to uplift your audience. Be comfortable with yourself and your material, and take pleasure in your performance.

Accept the terror that stalks presenters.

Transform it into thrill.

Appendix

TEASING SENTENCES

Several sleek sledges slithered sloppily sideways.

Gregg's Crinkle-Crisps crunch gratifyingly crisply.

The mask's task was to mask Mark in the middle of the Mayday Masque.

The fickle feelings of fair-weather friends' phase frank, friendly folk

With weasel words we winkled out one witless, wasted wizard.

Pumice particles plummeted past the palaeontologist's precarious perch.

Dubious ditties dully droned drowned the drunkard's deep despair.

Bubbling brooks babbled boisterously between bespangled boulders.

Gumdrops give gorging gluttons glutinous globs of glee.

Lovers linger longingly in leafy Loiterer's Lane.

My Nan mans Nan's Nan's van when Nan's Nan mans her old man's van.

Rhubarb and radish relish really restored Roger's restaurant's ratings.

Sunken, stranded ships strew several sheltered, shingled shores.

Treacherously taut tightropes train tortuously tensed tendons.

Wrong rang Wing and rang Wing wrong which really riled Wing.

FURTHER READING

Arredondo, Lani	*How to Present like a Pro*	McGraw Hill	(1991)
Burgess, Anthony	*A Mouthful of Air*	Hutchinson	(1992)
Crystal, David	*English as a Global Language*	Canto	(1998)
Greenbaum, Sidney	*The Oxford English Grammar*	OUP	(1996)
Honey, John	*Does Accent Matter?*	Faber and Faber	(1991)
Klepper, Michael M. with Gunther, Robert E.	*I'd Rather Die than give a Speech*	Irwin	(1998)
Ladefoged, Peter	*A Course in Phonetics*	Harcourt Brace	(1993)
McCallion, Michael	*The Voice Book*	Faber & Faber	(1988)
Rodenberg, Patsy	*The Right to Speak*	Methuen	(1992)
Wells, J.C.	*Pronunciation Dictionary*	Longman	(1990)

ABOUT THE AUTHOR

JANET HOWD. MA. PG dip.VS. ADVS is a voice coach who works with corporate, theatrical, legal, academic and private clients in the UK, Europe, North America and Australia. Her voice and presentation skills workshops are always tailored to the needs of individuals and, where appropriate, to fit the culture of specific organisations. She has written articles on voice and presentation for expert publications and for the Times Higher Educational Supplement. A professional singer and actress, she has worked extensively in theatre in the UK and has created leading roles in London, at the Edinburgh festival and for the BBC. She has performed as a recitalist worldwide, notably at the South Bank Concert Halls, the Wigmore Hall, the Carnegie Recital Hall and for BBC Radios 2 and 3. A skilled instructor, constantly alert to the concerns of others, her ideas on voice and presentational teaching have been successfully applied in situations ranging from small group work in small rooms to large gatherings in vast auditoriums. Her wide-ranging experience and first hand knowledge of vocal technique and of the mental and physical effort needed to deliver an effective message give a vital, practical edge to her coaching.

INDEX

F

Feedback 27–8, 64
Feynman, Richard 84–5
Flights 52
Flip charts 77
Fresh air 1

G

Glottal stop 10–11
    precautions with 10, 11
Grammar 24–5
Guiding tour groups 97–100
Gum ridge 17–18

H

Hand movements 28–30
Hard palate 16
Hoarseness 53
    glottal stop and 11
Humming 17
Humour 73

I

Illness 53
Imagery 57–8, 82, 83

J

Jargon 72
Jaw mobilisation 18–19, 44

L

Lap top computers 78
Lazy speech 22
Lectures 89–92
Lighting 75, 76
Lips 19–20
Loudness see Volume

M

Making an entrance 81
Material 70–1
    adding humour 73
    adding variety 72–3
    relevant material 70–1
    unavoidable topics 69–70
Memory 59
Metaphor 58
Microphones 79–80
Moving about 27–8
    see also Bodily movements
Muscle training 33, 86–7
    for volume 49–50
    lip muscles 19–20
    rib muscles 5–6

N

Nasal resonance 14–16
Neck 30–1
Nervousness 55, 56–7, 82
    imagery 57–8, 82
    relaxation 56–7
Notes, use of 78

O

Observation
    of TV presenters 62–3
    self-observation 60–2, 85–6
Outdoor conditions 98–9
Overheads 76
    see also Visual aids

P

Palate
    hard 16
    soft 14–15
Pauses 66